COOK WITH CONFIDENCE...

Spicy Beef and Broccoli Stir-Fry
Tomato Basil Chicken
Double Chocolate Cheesecake

AND SAVE MONEY TOO!

Shady Brook Farms® Turkey
Heinz Homestyle Gravy
Welch's Grape Juice
and much more—

Over $40 Worth of
Money-Saving Coupons

THE MONEY-$AVER$ COOKBOOK

COMPILED BY JODY CAMERON

AVON BOOKS ◆ NEW YORK

The owners of the companies offering coupons in *The
Money-Savers Cookbook* have agreed to honor all coupons indefinitely unless otherwise noted, and it is their
responsibility to do so. Celebrity Kitchen, Inc. and Avon
Books do not guarantee the price or availability of any
item, nor make representations or warranties regarding
the merchandise sold, and will not be responsible if any
establishment refuses to accept coupons.

THE MONEY-SAVERS COOKBOOK is an original publication of
Avon Books. This work has never before appeared in book form.

AVON BOOKS
A division of
The Hearst Corporation
1350 Avenue of the Americas
New York, New York 10019

Copyright © 1992 by Celebrity Kitchen, Inc.
Published by arrangement with the compiler
Library of Congress Catalog Card Number: 91-92064
ISBN: 0-380-76642-6

First Avon Books Printing: April 1992

AVON TRADEMARK REG. U.S. PAT. OFF. AND IN OTHER COUNTRIES,
MARCA REGISTRADA, HECHO EN U.S.A.

Printed in the U.S.A.

RA   10 9 8 7 6

In appreciation and thanks to
Susan Limato and Carolyn Malis

THE
MONEY-
$AVER$
COOKBOOK

Contents

Introduction

This unique cookbook contains more than 150 great-tasting recipes featuring your favorite brand name products . . . *and as a special money-saving bonus, you have over $40.00 in discount coupons toward the purchase of brand name products!*

Each brand name product has six to eight recipes for your cooking pleasure. The money-saving coupons apply to the brand name product in the recipe. Now, you have recipes and discount coupons *all in one place*! From this cookbook, you can select the desired recipe and *save money using the discount coupon* in the back of the cookbook for the brand name product mentioned.

Take a moment to look at some of the fabulous recipes in this cookbook. They were all created by the top professionals at the participating brand name companies and designed to win you compliments at home.

The following list is a small sampling of the many delicious recipes you can prepare. *And remember to use the money-savers discount coupon in the back of this cookbook when you purchase the brand name product!*

Product	*Recipe*
Adolph's® Marinade in Minutes	Spicy Steak Oriental
Carnation® Evaporated Milk	Five Minute Fudge
Carnation® Sweetened Condensed Milk	Chocolate Macaroon Squares
Cool Whip® Whipped Topping	Strawberry Ribbon Cheesecake
Grandma's® Molasses	Easy Glazed Ham
Heinz Chili Sauce	Shrimp Sauté
Heinz HomeStyle Gravy	Tex-Mex Chili Beef
Heinz Tomato Ketchup	Bayou Jambalaya
Heinz Vinegar	Polynesian Chicken
Kretschmer® Wheat Germ	Crunchy Green Bean Casserole
Lea & Perrins Worcestershire Sauce	Gingered Broccoli
Nabisco® Cream of Wheat	Peach Melba Mold
Nestlé® Toll House Chocolate Morsels	Chocolate Peanut Buddy Bars
Reynolds Cooking Bags	Today's Easy Beef Stew
Royal® Gelatin and Pudding and No Bake Pie Mix	Two-Tone Fruit Pie
Seneca Frozen Cranberry Juice	Breakfast Beverage
Shady Brook Farms® Turkey	Turkey Creole
Welch's Grape Juice	Tropical Surprise
Welch's Spreads	Naturally Sweet Snack Bars

Coupon Clipping Saves $ $ $

Money-saving coupons can save the average shopper $20.00 and more off the weekly budget. Take advantage of these coupons and watch your savings multiply.

Always try to have your coupons organized. Try to devote as little time as possible to the coupon clipping project so that it doesn't become a nuisance.

- File your coupons by category the way the products are displayed in the supermarket. This helps you find the coupon products quickly and easily.

- Read the coupon carefully. Do you have to buy one or more of the same product to get the coupon savings? Note the product size. Check the expiration date. Some coupons are valid for a short time only. A coupon that has *no expiration date* is a true value. You can purchase the product *anytime*! Most of the money-saving coupons in this cookbook have no expiration date or dates that extend for two years or more.

- Don't be tempted to buy a product simply because you have a coupon.

- Discard coupons you don't intend to use.

- Check for coupons on product packages. If you have a coupon to use now for that item, you'll also have one from the package to use for your next purchase of the same product.

- If the supermarket is out of the item, bring the coupon to the manager's desk for a rain check.

Aside from food savings, *you have additional savings on brand name products for the kitchen*!

Big Savings from Farberware!

Farberware, Inc., offers the following mail-in coupons for their cookware.

Farberware® Indoor Smokeless Grill	$5.00 off coupon
Farberware® Electric Skillet	$5.00 off coupon
Farberware® Electric Wok	$5.00 off coupon
Farberware® Convection Oven	$10.00 off coupon

Coupons on pages 197.

Big Savings from Sears!

Sears offers, at point of purchase, a $10.00 off coupon for any table appliance in the Kenmore Choice line such as:

The Exclusive "Brew for Two" 12-cup Coffee-maker

Deluxe 14-Speed Blender

14-Speed Hand Mixer

Toaster Oven Broiler

Food Processor and others

Coupon on page 205.

Shopping Tips

Food shopping should be a once or twice a week event. The more trips you make to the supermarket, the more money you'll spend and there goes the budget.

When you make out your shopping list, try to organize it as follows:

1. packaged and canned goods
2. fresh fruits and vegetables
3. refrigerator and freezer items

Refrigerator and freezer items are last on the list because cold foods should be out of the store for as short a time as possible.

Now when you get to the checkout, your groceries will be packed in the order in which you shopped. Unpacking your groceries when you get home will be much easier.

On your shopping list, circle the product for which you have a coupon. By doing so, you won't have to constantly refer to the coupon as you shop.

Avoid impulse buying. *It can be costly!*

My Favorite Recipes
in *The Money-Savers Cookbook*

Title	Page #

Title	*Page #*

THE
MONEY-
$AVER$
COOKBOOK

Money-Saving
Recipes

Tasty Soups

CHEDDAR VEGETABLE POTTAGE

Makes 4 servings

10-ounce package frozen peas and carrots
10½-ounce can condensed cheddar cheese soup

1½ cups milk
¼ cup Kretschmer® wheat germ
½ teaspoon instant minced onion

Prepare frozen peas and carrots according to package directions. Do not drain. Add soup. Stir well to blend.

Add remaining ingredients. Heat just to boiling, stirring occasionally.

FISH STEW, SOUTHERN STYLE

Makes 4 to 6 servings

1 cup sliced
   onions
2 tablespoons
   vegetable oil
1¾-pound can
   tomatoes,
   cut into bite-
   sized pieces
½ cup Heinz
   tomato
   ketchup
1 tablespoon
   Worcestershire
   sauce

1 teaspoon sugar
½ teaspoon salt
⅛ teaspoon pepper
2 bay leaves
⅛ teaspoon hot
   pepper sauce
   (optional)
1 pound fish fillets,
   cut into bite-
   sized pieces
Hot cooked rice

In large saucepan or Dutch oven, sauté onions in oil until tender. Stir in tomatoes and next 6 ingredients. Simmer, uncovered, 30 minutes, stirring occasionally.

Add fish; simmer 10 to 15 minutes or until fish flakes easily with fork. Remove bay leaves. Thicken sauce, with flour-water mixture if desired.

Serve stew in soup bowls over or topped with a mound of rice.

Note: Flour-water thickening mixture is made with 2 tablespoons flour and ¼ cup water.

RICE AND CHEESE CHOWDER

Makes 8 servings

½ pound bacon, cut into ½-inch pieces
1 tablespoon vegetable oil
¼ cup chopped onion
⅓ cup all-purpose flour
½ cup wild rice
½ cup brown rice
4½ cups water

1¾ cups (14½-ounce can) chicken broth
1½ cups (12-ounce can) *undiluted* Carnation® evaporated milk
2½ cups grated American cheese
1–2 tablespoons chopped fresh parsley (optional)

In large skillet, cook bacon until crisp. Drain on paper towels; set aside.

In large saucepan, heat oil over medium-high heat; sauté onions for about 2 minutes or until translucent. Remove from heat. Stir in flour. Add rices, water, and broth. Return to heat; bring to a boil. Reduce heat; simmer for 35 to 40 minutes or until rice is tender, stirring frequently.

Stir in evaporated milk, bacon, and cheese. Heat until cheese is melted. Garnish with chopped parsley, if desired.

SWEDISH COLD FRUIT SOUP

Makes 6 to 8 servings

1½ cups Welch's purple grape juice

1½ cups apple juice

Generous dash allspice

Generous dash ground cardamom

½ cup cantaloupe balls

½ cup coarsely chopped unpared apple

1 medium orange, sectioned, cut in chunks

8-ounce can peach slices, undrained (or fresh peaches), coarsely chopped

Combine all ingredients. Chill well. Serve in individual hollowed-out cantaloupe halves or orange shells.

OLD-FASHIONED BEAN SOUP

Makes 10 servings

6 cups water
1 pound navy
   beans, washed
   and sorted
8 cups water
2 large meaty
   smoked ham
   hocks
2 medium onions,
   chopped

2 medium carrots,
   chopped
2 stalks celery,
   chopped
1 bay leaf
1 teaspoon salt
¼ teaspoon pepper
½ cup Heinz tomato
   ketchup

In large saucepan, bring 6 cups water to a boil.
Add beans; boil 2 minutes. Remove from heat;
cover and let stand 1 hour.

Drain beans, discarding water. Combine beans,
8 cups water, and next 7 ingredients. Cover; simmer
2½ to 3 hours or until beans are tender.

Discard bay leaf. Cut meat from bones; return
meat to soup. Stir in ketchup; heat.

TODAY'S EASY BEEF SOUP

Makes 4 to 6 servings

¼ cup flour
1 large (14 by 20 inch) Reynolds oven cooking bag
14½-ounce can Italian-style stewed tomatoes, undrained

1 envelope onion soup mix
¼ teaspoon pepper
2 pounds beef for stew, fat trimmed
4 medium carrots, cut in 2-inch pieces
4 medium potatoes, quartered

Preheat oven to 325° F. Shake flour in oven cooking bag; place in 9 by 13 by 2-inch baking pan. Add tomatoes, onion soup mix, and pepper to bag. Squeeze bag to blend ingredients. Add beef and vegetables to bag. Turn bag to coat ingredients. Arrange ingredients in an even layer. Close bag with nylon tie; cut six ½-inch slits in top. Bake 1½ to 2 hours or until beef is tender.

Note: Sauce will cause the top of the bag to darken in color. This is a normal reaction and does not indicate burning.

SWISS BROCCOLI SOUP

Makes 4 servings

2 tablespoons minced onion
1 tablespoon butter or margarine
12-ounce jar Heinz HomeStyle chicken gravy

1¼ cups milk
10-ounce package frozen chopped broccoli, cooked, drained
1 cup shredded Swiss cheese
Dash salt
Dash pepper

Sauté onion in butter until tender. Stir in gravy, milk, and broccoli; heat slowly, stirring occasionally. Add cheese, salt, and pepper; heat until cheese is melted, stirring frequently.

Perfect Fish

BAYOU JAMBALAYA

Makes 4 to 6 servings

1 medium
onion, sliced
½ cup chopped
green
pepper
1 clove garlic,
minced
1 cup uncooked
white rice
2 tablespoons
butter or
margarine
1 cup Heinz
tomato ketchup
2¼ cups water

1 tablespoon Heinz
vinegar
⅛ teaspoons black
pepper
⅛ teaspoon red
pepper
1 medium tomato,
coarsely
chopped
1 cup cubed
cooked ham
½ pound raw
shrimp,
deveined and
shelled

In large skillet, sauté first 4 ingredients in butter
until onion is transparent. Stir in ketchup and remaining ingredients except shrimp. Cover; simmer
20 to 25 minutes or until rice is tender.

Add shrimp; simmer uncovered 3 to 5 minutes or until shrimp turn pink, stirring occasionally.

Microwave Directions: Place onion, green pepper, garlic, and butter in 3-quart casserole. Cover dish with lid or vented plastic wrap; microwave on high 3 to 4 minutes, stirring once. Stir in rice, ketchup, water, vinegar, black pepper, red pepper, tomato, and ham. Cover; microwave on high 10 to 12 minutes or until mixture comes to a boil. Microwave on medium (50 percent) 18 to 20 minutes until rice is cooked, stirring once. Stir in shrimp; cover. Microwave on high 2 to 3 minutes or until shrimp turn pink. Let stand, covered, 5 minutes before serving.

LIGHT AND SAUCY SHRIMP

Makes 3 to 4 servings

1 cup chopped onion
½ cup coarsely chopped green pepper
2 cloves garlic, minced
¼ cup water
1 teaspoon sugar
¼ teaspoon fines herbes
⅛ teaspoon pepper

14½-ounce can stewed tomatoes (no added salt), cut into bite-sized pieces
¼ cup Heinz apple cider vinegar
¾ pound medium-sized raw shrimp, shelled and deveined
1 tablespoon cornstarch
1 tablespoon water
Hot cooked rice

In 2-quart saucepan, combine first 7 ingredients; simmer, covered, 10 minutes or until onions are tender. Stir in tomatoes and vinegar; simmer, covered, 15 minutes, stirring occasionally.

Add shrimp; simmer an additional 5 minutes or until shrimp turn pink, stirring occasionally. Combine cornstarch and water; stir into tomato mixture. Simmer until thickened, stirring constantly.

Serve over rice.

SOUTHWEST TUNA SALAD

Makes 4 servings

12½-ounce can
  tuna,
  drained,
  flaked into
  large pieces
2 medium
  tomatoes,
  cut into
  chunks
1 medium
  avocado,
  peeled, cut
  into chunks
½ cup sliced
  green onion

¼ cup chopped fresh
  parsley or
  cilantro
¼ cup Heinz
  distilled white
  vinegar
¼ cup vegetable oil
Dash salt
Dash pepper
Lettuce cups
Sour cream
Tortilla chips
Avocado slices
  (optional)

In large bowl, lightly combine first 5 ingredients. To make dressing, combine vinegar, oil, salt, and pepper in a jar; cover and shake vigorously. Pour dressing over tuna mixture; toss gently to coat.

Spoon salad into lettuce cups; top with dollop of sour cream. Serve salad with tortilla chips. Garnish with avocado slices, if desired.

SHRIMP SAUTÉ

Makes 4 servings

½ cup Heinz chili sauce
½ cup apple juice
1 tablespoon soy sauce
2 teaspoons cornstarch
⅛ teaspoon hot pepper sauce
2 cups broccoli florets
1 cup quartered fresh mushrooms

1 small green or red bell pepper, cut into thin strips
8-ounce can sliced water chestnuts, drained
2 tablespoons vegetable oil
1 pound medium-sized raw shrimp, shelled and deveined
Hot buttered rice or couscous

Combine first 5 ingredients; set aside.

In large skillet, sauté broccoli, mushrooms, pepper, and water chestnuts in oil 1 to 2 minutes or until vegetables are tender-crisp; remove from skillet.

Sauté shrimp 2 to 3 minutes, adding more oil if necessary. Stir in chili sauce mixture; heat until thickened. Return vegetables to skillet; heat, stirring to coat.

Serve with rice or couscous.

FISH AND CHIPS

Makes 4 to 6 servings

2 large potatoes, peeled and cut into ½ by ½ by 3-inch strips
1 cup flour
1 teaspoon baking powder
1 teaspoon salt
1 cup flat beer

1 tablespoon vegetable oil
1 pound flounder or sole fillets
¼ cup flour
2 cups vegetable oil or vegetable shortening

In medium bowl, soak potatoes in cold water about 30 minutes.

Meanwhile, in second bowl, combine flour, baking powder, and salt. Make a well in the center of flour mixture. Add beer and 1 tablespoon oil. Mix until smooth.

On plate, coat fish with remaining ¼ cup flour. In Farberware® electric skillet, heat 2 cups oil with heat control set at 375° F. When light goes out, dip fish into batter. Fry 4 fillets at a time for 3 minutes on each side or until golden brown. Remove fish with slotted spoon; drain on paper towel. Keep fish warm. Repeat until all fillets have been cooked.

Drain potatoes. Pat dry. Heat oil remaining in skillet with heat control set at 375° F. When light goes out, add half of the potato strips; cook 5 to 7 minutes. Remove from skillet. Drain on paper towels. Sprinkle with salt.

Serve fish with tartar sauce.

STUFFED FLOUNDER

Makes 4 to 6 servings

2 pounds flounder or sole fillets

8-ounce package frozen chopped spinach

¼ cup butter or margarine

1 cup chopped onions

⅓ cup pignolia nuts (pine nuts)

¼ cup Parmesan cheese

1 teaspoon basil

1 teaspoon salt

½ teaspoon pepper

1 egg, beaten

1 cup dry white wine

1 cup fish or chicken broth

1 bay leaf

Wash and dry fillets.

Cook spinach according to package directions. Set aside.

In Farberware® electric skillet melt butter with heat control set at 350° F. Sauté onions and pignolia nuts about 3 or 4 minutes.

In large bowl, combine sautéed onion mixture, spinach, cheese, basil, salt, pepper, and egg. Mix well.

Place about 2 tablespoons filling mixture onto each fillet. Fold ends over filling. Roll up jelly-roll style. Secure with wooden picks.

In Farberware® electric skillet, simmer white wine, broth, and bay leaf with heat control set at 250° F. Carefully add fish rolls. Cover. Cook at 250° F. until fish flakes easily with fork, about 15 to 20 minutes.

FISH WITH VERMOUTH SAUCE

Makes 4 servings

2 tablespoons
  butter or
  margarine
4 scallions,
  thinly sliced
1½ tablespoons
  all-purpose
  flour

½ cup dry
  vermouth
1 cup milk
1 egg yolk
¼ teaspoon salt
1¼ pound fish fillets
  or fish steaks

Preheat Farberware® smokeless indoor grill to 350° F with greased rack in high position.

In small saucepan, melt butter over low heat. Add scallions and cook until tender. Add flour and continue to cook until smooth, stirring constantly.

In a bowl, mix together vermouth, milk, egg yolk, and salt; add to flour mixture. Cook over low heat until thickened, stirring constantly. Keep warm.

Place fish on rack on grill; broil 10 to 12 minutes for fish fillets or 30 to 35 minutes for fish steaks or until fish flakes easily with fork, turning once using a spatula.

Serve fish with sauce.

GRILLED SWORDFISH BROCHETTES

Makes 10 skewers

1 package Adolph's® Marinade in Minutes, lemon pepper flavor

⅔ cup water

2 tablespoons lemon juice

2 tablespoons olive oil

2 tablespoons honey

2 tablespoons chopped fresh dill

1 tablespoon Dijon mustard

1 teaspoon Lea & Perrins white wine Worcestershire sauce

3–4 drops hot pepper sauce (optional)

2 pounds swordfish steak, trimmed and cut into large chunks

1 large red bell pepper, cut into 1-inch cubes

14¾-ounce jar marinated artichoke hearts, drained

Hot, cooked rice

Prepare grill or preheat broiler.

In a medium bowl, thoroughly combine marinade mix with water, lemon juice, olive oil, honey, dill, mustard, Worcestershire sauce, and pepper sauce.

Add swordfish cubes and marinate 15 minutes. Alternate swordfish, red pepper, and artichoke hearts on 8-inch skewers. Grill or broil about 6 inches from heat, 6 minutes per side or until done. Baste occasionally with remaining marinade.

Serve over rice.

POACHED FISH

Makes 6 servings

6 fillets of sole	1 tablespoon
20-ounce can	cornstarch
unsweetened	¼ cup sliced
cubed	almonds
pineapple	Clusters of
1 cup Welch's	seedless green
white grape	grapes, for
juice	garnish
½ teaspoon salt	Sprigs of
¼ teaspoon	watercress, for
ground	garnish
cumin	

Roll up fish fillets and secure with toothpicks.

Drain pineapple, reserving 1½ cups pineapple cubes and ¼ cup pineapple juice.

Place grape juice, salt, and cumin in large skillet; add fish fillets. Bring to a boil; reduce heat. Cover and simmer gently 12 to 15 minutes or until fish tests done. Remove fish to warmed serving platter.

Blend cornstarch with reserved pineapple juice; stir into grape juice mixture and cook until thickened and smooth. Add reserved pineapple cubes and cook just until heated through.

Pour sauce over fillets. Sprinkle with almonds. Garnish with grapes and watercress.

THREE PEPPER SAUCE OVER FISH

Makes 4 servings

1 cup julienned
    red, green,
    and yellow
    peppers
1 cup sliced
    mushrooms
½ cup chopped
    onion
1 clove garlic, minced
1 tablespoon olive
    oil
2 tablespoons all-
    purpose flour
¾ cup undiluted
    Carnation®
    evaporated
    skimmed or
    lowfat milk

¼ cup water
2 tablespoons dry
    white wine
¼ teaspoon salt
1 tablespoon
    slivered fresh
    basil leaves or
    ½ teaspoon
    dried basil
    leaves
12 ounces fresh fish
    fillets or steaks

In medium skillet, sauté peppers, mushrooms, onions, and garlic in oil over medium heat, about 6 minutes or until excess moisture is evaporated. Stir in flour; cook, stirring constantly, 1 minute. Gradually add milk, water, wine, and salt. Heat, stirring constantly, until mixture comes to a full boil and thickens. Stir in basil. Keep warm.

Lightly brush both sides of fish with oil. Place on broiler rack, tucking under any thin ends. Broil 6 inches from heat without turning, about 4 to 6 minutes, or until fish flakes easily with a fork.

Serve warm sauce over fish.

CALIFORNIA FISH BROIL

Makes 4 servings

1¼ pounds fresh fish fillets
½ cup Heinz chili sauce
½ cup orange juice
¼ cup olive oil

2 tablespoons lemon juice
1 tablespoon Worcestershire sauce
Chopped fresh parsley

Cut fish into 4 serving-size portions; place in shallow dish.

Combine chili sauce, orange juice, oil, lemon juice, and Worcestershire sauce in small bowl; pour over fish. Cover; refrigerate for 30 to 60 minutes.

Place fish in greased broiler pan. Broil 4 inches from heat source, allowing 10 minutes per inch of thickness. Fish is cooked when it turns opaque and just flakes when tested with fork.

Sprinkle parsley over fish before serving.

Main Meat Dishes

BRAISED BEEF WITH RICE

Makes 4 servings

1 tablespoon shortening
1 pound beef chuck, cut into 1-inch pieces
1 clove garlic, minced
1 teaspoon salt
2 cups water
½ cup Heinz tomato ketchup
1 medium onion, sliced
2 tablespoons minced parsley
⅔ cup uncooked rice

Melt shortening in large skillet. Add garlic and beef. Brown beef well on all sides. Sprinkle with salt. Stir in water, ketchup, onion slices, and parsley. Cover; simmer 15 minutes.

Stir in rice. Cover; simmer 25 minutes or until beef is tender and rice has absorbed liquid, stirring occasionally.

TERIYAKI STEAK

Makes 4 servings

¼ cup soy sauce
¼ cup dry sherry
2 tablespoons
    brown sugar
1 tablespoon
    vegetable oil

2 cloves garlic,
    minced
¼ teaspoon ginger
¼ teaspoon pepper
    2-pound flank
    steak

In bowl, combine all ingredients except flank steak. Mix thoroughly. Pour mixture into a shallow pan. Add flank steak. Turn to coat with marinade. Cover meat and refrigerate overnight.

Preheat Farberware® smokeless indoor grill with rack in low position to 350° F. Remove steak from marinade and place on rack. Discard marinade. Broil 7 to 10 minutes each side for rare; 12 to 14 minutes for medium; 15 to 17 minutes for well done.

BEEF STROGANOFF

Makes 4 to 6 servings

1½ pounds boneless sirloin, cut into 2 by ¾ by ⅜-inch strips

2 tablespoons vegetable oil

1 cup coarsely chopped onions

12-ounce jar Heinz HomeStyle mushroom gravy

2 tablespoons red wine (optional)

1 tablespoon tomato paste

Salt and pepper

⅓ cup sour cream

Hot buttered noodles

Chopped fresh parsley

In large skillet, quickly brown meat in oil. Add onions; cook until limp. Stir in gravy, wine, and tomato paste. Season with salt and pepper. Cover; simmer 10 to 20 minutes, or until meat is tender.

Remove from heat, slowly stir in sour cream. Serve over noodles. Garnish with parsley.

TEX-MEX CHILI BEEF

Makes 4 servings

1-pound flank steak, halved lengthwise, cut diagonally into ⅛-inch-thick slices
1 cup sliced onions
1–2 tablespoons chili powder
2 tablespoons vegetable oil

12-ounce jar Heinz HomeStyle brown gravy
⅓ cup water
Warm corn muffins, split
Monterey Jack or Cheddar cheese (optional)

In large skillet, stir-fry steak, onions, and chili powder in oil 5 minutes; reduce heat. Stir in gravy and water; simmer 3 minutes.

To serve, spoon beef mixture over muffins. Top with shredded Monterey Jack or Cheddar cheese, if desired.

GINGERED BEEF

Makes 4 servings

1 pound boneless beef sirloin steak, cut ½-inch thick	1 cup sliced mushrooms
⅓ cup diagonally sliced celery	1 cup snow pea pods
1 small red bell pepper, cut into strips	12-ounce jar Heinz HomeStyle brown gravy
1–2 teaspoons grated fresh ginger	⅓ cup sliced water chestnuts
2 tablespoons vegetable oil, divided	4 green onions, cut into ½-inch lengths
	1 tablespoon soy sauce
	Hot cooked rice

Cut steak across the grain into ⅛-inch strips; set aside.

In preheated large skillet or wok, stir-fry celery, red bell pepper, and ginger in 1 tablespoon oil for 1 minute. Add mushrooms and snow peas and stir-fry 1 to 2 minutes longer or until vegetables are tender-crisp; remove from skillet.

Stir-fry beef in remaining 1 tablespoon oil. Add gravy, water chestnuts, onions, and soy sauce. Return vegetables to skillet; heat.

Serve over rice.

SPICY BEEF AND BROCCOLI STIR-FRY

Makes 4 servings

½ cup Heinz chili sauce

3 tablespoons water

2 tablespoons soy sauce

1 tablespoon cornstarch

½ teaspoon ginger

½ teaspoon crushed red pepper flakes

1 pound boneless sirloin steak, cut into ½-inch strips

2 tablespoons vegetable oil, divided

1½ cups broccoli florets

1 small green or red bell pepper, cut into strips

1 small onion, sliced

8-ounce can sliced water chestnuts, drained

Hot cooked rice

Combine chili sauce, water, soy sauce, cornstarch, ginger, and crushed red pepper in small bowl; set aside.

In preheated large skillet or wok, stir-fry beef strips in 1 tablespoon oil about 3 minutes or until browned. Remove and set aside.

Add remaining 1 tablespoon oil to wok, stir-fry broccoli, green pepper, onion, and water chestnuts 3 to 4 minutes or until vegetables are tender-crisp. Stir in reserved chili sauce mixture; cook until thickened. Stir in browned beef strips and heat 1 to 2 minutes or until hot.

Serve over rice.

SWEET AND SOUR MEATBALLS

Makes 40 minimeatballs

1 pound lean
  ground beef
1 cup soft bread
  crumbs
1 egg, slightly
  beaten
2 tablespoons
  minced onion
2 tablespoons milk

1 clove garlic,
  minced
½ teaspoon salt
⅛ teaspoon pepper
1 tablespoon
  vegetable oil
⅔ cup Heinz chili
  sauce
⅔ cup red currant
  or grape jelly

Combine first 8 ingredients; form into 40 bite-sized meatballs, using a full teaspoon for each. Brown meatballs lightly in oil. Cover; cook over low heat for 5 minutes. Drain excess fat.

Combine chili sauce and jelly; pour over meatballs. Heat, stirring occasionally, until jelly is melted. Simmer 10 to 12 minutes until sauce has thickened, basting occasionally.

Note: To serve as a main dish, form meat mixture into 20 meatballs. Cook as directed above.

TIME-TO-SPARE RIBS

Makes 4 to 6 servings

¼ cup flour
1 large (14 by 20-inch) Reynolds oven cooking bag
1½ cups barbecue sauce

½ cup chopped onion
½ cup chopped green pepper
3½ pounds pork spareribs, fat trimmed

Preheat oven to 325° F.

Shake flour into cooking bag; place bag in 9 by 13 by 2-inch baking pan. Add barbecue sauce, onion, and green pepper to bag. Squeeze bag to blend ingredients.

Cut ribs in serving size pieces; place in bag. Turn bag to coat ribs with sauce. Arrange ribs in an even layer in bag. Close bag with nylon tie; cut six ½-inch slits in top. Bake 1½ hours or until ribs are tender.

Note: Sauce will cause the top of the bag to darken in color. This is a normal reaction and does not indicate burning.

Country-Style Ribs

Substitute 3½ pounds country-style pork ribs for spareribs.

Barbecue Beef Short Ribs

Substitute 4 pounds beef short ribs for spareribs.

CHILLY DAY CHILI

Makes 10 servings

2 medium onions, chopped
1 green pepper, chopped
2 tablespoons vegetable oil
2 pounds lean ground beef
16-ounce can tomatoes, cut into bite-sized pieces
15-ounce can tomato sauce
½ cup Heinz tomato ketchup
1–2 tablespoons chili powder
1 teaspoon salt
¼ teaspoon pepper
two 15½ ounce-cans red kidney beans, partially drained

In large saucepan or Dutch oven, sauté onions and green pepper in oil until tender. Add beef; cook until beef loses pink color, stirring occasionally. Drain excess fat.

Add tomatoes and next 5 ingredients. Simmer, uncovered, 30 minutes, stirring occasionally.

Add kidney beans; simmer an additional 15 minutes.

FIESTA BEEF PIE

Makes 4 servings

1 cup chopped onions
1 large green pepper, coarsely chopped
1 clove garlic, minced
1 tablespoon vegetable oil
1 pound lean ground beef
1 cup Heinz tomato ketchup

1 medium tomato, coarsely chopped
1 tablespoon minced jalapeño pepper
2 teaspoons chili powder
8½-ounce package corn muffin mix
½ cup shredded Monterey Jack cheese

Preheat oven to 375° F.

In large skillet, sauté onions, green pepper, and garlic in oil until onions are tender-crisp. Add beef and cook until meat is browned; drain excess fat. Stir in ketchup and next 3 ingredients; heat to boiling.

Meanwhile, prepare corn muffin mix following package directions. Spoon batter around edges of greased 8-inch-square baking dish. Carefully spoon meat mixture into center of dish, keeping batter toward outside edge of dish. Bake for 20 minutes.

Top meat mixture with cheese; bake an additional 5 minutes. Let stand 5 minutes before serving.

SPICY STEAK ORIENTAL

Makes 6 servings

1 package
Adolph's®
Marinade in
Minutes,
garlic dijon
flavor
½ cup water
2 tablespoons soy
sauce
2 tablespoons
vinegar

1 tablespoon
lemon juice
1 teaspoon minced
fresh garlic
1 teaspoon minced
fresh ginger
½ teaspoon hot
sesame oil
1½ pounds flank
steak

Preheat grill or broiler.

In a shallow bowl, thoroughly combine contents of marinade package with water, soy sauce, vinegar, lemon juice, garlic, ginger, and sesame oil. Place steak in marinade, pierce deeply with a fork. Marinate 15 minutes, turning occasionally.

Grill or broil steak 7 minutes per side for medium. Baste with remaining marinade during cooking.

BEEF SATAY WITH PEANUT SAUCE

Makes 6 servings

2 pounds flank steak, sliced diagonally across the grain into ½-inch slices and pounded thin
1 package Adolph's® Marinade in Minutes
1 cup hot water

2 tablespoons sesame oil
1 tablespoon lemon juice
1 tablespoon soy sauce
1 teaspoon minced fresh garlic
¼ teaspoon hot chili oil
½ cup creamy-style peanut butter
Hot, cooked rice

Preheat broiler.

On small wooden skewers, thread 1 slice beef lengthwise, piercing meat 4 to 5 times for each skewer. Repeat, making 12 to 15 ribbon-like skewers. Set aside.

In a medium bowl, thoroughly combine contents of marinade package with hot water, sesame oil, lemon juice, soy sauce, garlic, and hot chili oil. Add peanut butter; mix until thoroughly blended. Dip skewered meat in marinade mixture on both sides to coat thoroughly. Place in single layer on broiler pan with rack. Marinate 15 minutes.

Broil 5 minutes per side, or until thoroughly cooked. Baste with remaining marinade mixture while meat is broiling.

Serve over hot cooked rice.

SPANISH SKILLET DINNER

Makes 4 servings

½ pound sirloin steak, cubed

2 teaspoons ground cumin

1–2 teaspoons chili powder

2 tablespoons olive oil

½ cup chopped onion

½ cup chopped green bell pepper

14½-ounce can no-salt-added whole tomatoes, drained and chopped (reserve liquid)

Water

1 cup quick cooking brown rice, uncooked

½ cup Kretschmer® wheat germ

1 tablespoon chopped fresh cilantro (optional)

Sprinkle steak with cumin and chili powder. Heat oil in large heavy skillet; brown steak over medium heat. Add onion and green pepper; cook about 2 minutes, stirring constantly.

Add enough water to reserved tomato liquid to equal 1¾ cups. Add to skillet; bring to a boil. Add rice; reduce heat. Cover and simmer about 10 minutes, or until most of the liquid is absorbed.

Stir in tomatoes and wheat germ. Remove from heat; cover and let stand until all liquid is absorbed.

Stir before serving. Top with fresh cilantro. Serve immediately.

STIR-FRIED PORK AND VEGGIES

Makes 4 servings

¼ cup Grandma's®
   molasses
   (Gold Label)
2 tablespoons
   sherry
2 tablespoons soy
   sauce
1 tablespoon
   hoisin sauce

1 pound boneless
   pork, cut
   into thin
   strips
2 tablespoons oil

1 cup diagonally
   cut fresh
   asparagus or
   pea pods
1 cup (2 medium)
   diagonally
   sliced carrots
2 tablespoons
   cornstarch
¾ cup beef broth or
   water
Toasted sesame
   seeds, if desired
Cooked vermicelli

In medium bowl, combine molasses, sherry, soy sauce, and hoisin sauce; blend well. Add pork; stir to coat. Cover; refrigerate 1 to 2 hours or overnight.

In large skillet, heat 1 tablespoon oil. Stir-fry asparagus and carrots 3 to 5 minutes or until tender-crisp. Remove vegetables from pan. Add 1 table-spoon oil and pork mixture to pan. Stir-fry 5 minutes or until brown.

In small bowl, combine cornstarch and broth; blend well. Stir into pork mixture; cook until mixture thickens, stirring constantly. Return vegetables to pan; thoroughly heat.

Sprinkle with sesame seeds. Serve with vermicelli or oriental noodles.

PORK PICCATA

Makes 4 servings

1 pound pork
   tenderloin or
   boneless loin,
   cut into ¼-
   inch slices
1 tablespoon
   vegetable oil
12-ounce jar Heinz
   HomeStyle
   pork gravy

2 tablespoons water
1 tablespoon lemon
   juice
8 thin lemon slices
1 tablespoon drained
   capers

In large skillet, quickly sauté pork in oil until
lightly browned and cooked; remove and set aside.

In same skillet, stir in gravy, water, and lemon
juice; heat until bubbly. Add lemon, capers, and
reserved pork; heat.

Garnish with chopped parsley and serve with rice,
if desired.

STUFFED PORK CHOPS

Makes 4 servings

4 rib pork
   chops, cut
   1¼ inches
   thick and
   slit for stuffing
1½ cups prepared
   stuffing mix
   (any flavor)

1 tablespoon
   vegetable oil
Salt and pepper
12-ounce bottle
   Heinz chili
   sauce

Preheat oven to 350° F.

Trim excess fat from chops. Place stuffing in pockets of chops; secure with toothpicks. Brown chops in oil; season with salt and pepper.

Place chops in 2-quart oblong baking dish. Pour chili sauce over chops. Cover dish with foil; bake for 30 minutes. Stir sauce to blend; turn and baste chops. Cover; bake an additional 30 to 40 minutes or until chops are tender.

Remove toothpicks from chops. Skim excess fat from sauce; spoon over chops.

PORK CHOPS NAPOLI

Makes 6 servings

6 rib pork chops, cut ¾-inch thick
1 tablespoon vegetable oil
1 medium onion, sliced
16-ounce can tomatoes, cut into bite-sized pieces

⅔ cup Heinz tomato ketchup
½ teaspoon dried oregano leaves, crushed
½ teaspoon garlic salt
⅛ teaspoon pepper
Hot cooked noodles

In large skillet, brown chops in oil; remove.

In same skillet, sauté onion until tender. Combine tomatoes and next 4 ingredients; pour into skillet. Return chops to skillet. Cover; simmer 20 to 25 minutes, basting occasionally.

If thicker sauce is desired, gradually stir in mixture of equal parts flour and water, simmering until thickened.

To serve, spoon sauce over chops and noodles.

ROAST LOIN OF PORK

Makes 6 servings

1 tablespoon vegetable oil	½ teaspoon paprika
2½ pounds lean, boneless pork loin	½ cup sliced onion
1 tablespoon flour	1 cup Lea & Perrins white wine Worcestershire sauce, divided

Preheat oven to 350° F.

In a large uncovered pot, heat oil. Sprinkle pork roast with flour and paprika and brown in the hot oil. Arrange onion slices on top and around meat and pour ½ cup Worcestershire sauce over.

Roast 1 hour or until done, basting occasionally with the remaining Worcestershire sauce.

Serve sliced, with buttered seasonal vegetables.

PAN-SEARED LEMON LAMB CHOPS

Makes 2 to 4 servings

4 lamb chops (shoulder chops for economy; loin chops for special tenderness)
2 tablespoons butter
Juice of ½ lemon
¼ teaspoon freshly ground pepper
2 tablespoons Lea & Perrins Worcestershire sauce
¼ cup chopped parsley

Slit outer fat of chops to prevent curling. Heat skillet; add 1 tablespoon of butter, tilting pan to coat bottom. Brown chops over fairly high heat, about 4 minutes each side for medium-rare.

Add remaining ingredients (including remaining butter) and heat, spooning the sauce over chops to coat.

EASY GLAZED HAM

Makes 8 to 10 servings

½ cup Grandma's® molasses (Gold Label)
3 ounces frozen orange juice concentrate, thawed
4–5 pound fully cooked boneless ham

Preheat oven to 325° F.

In small bowl, combine molasses and orange juice; set aside.

With sharp knife score top of ham in crisscross pattern. Place in shallow roasting pan. Bake for 1½ hours or until fully heated. During last 30 minutes of baking, brush ham with glaze.

PARTY HAM LOAF

Makes 8 to 10 servings

1½ pounds ground pork
1 pound ground smoked ham
1 cup soft bread crumbs
1 cup milk
2 eggs

1 cup firmly packed light brown sugar
½ cup Heinz apple cider vinegar
½ cup water
1 tablespoon prepared mustard

Preheat oven to 350° F.

Combine first 5 ingredients; shape into a 12 by 4 by 2-inch loaf in a 9 by 13 by 2-inch baking pan.

Blend sugar and remaining ingredients; pour over loaf. Bake for 2 hours, basting occasionally.

Skim excess fat from sauce; serve sauce with ham loaf.

SAUCY VEAL AND VEGETABLES

Makes 4 servings

2 cups quartered
  fresh
  mushrooms
1 cup julienned
  carrots
1 small zucchini,
  halved
  lengthwise,
  cut into ¼-
  inch slices
4 green onions,
  cut into ½-
  inch pieces
½ teaspoon dried
  basil, crushed
½ teaspoon salt
¼ teaspoon
  pepper

¼ teaspoon dried
  oregano,
  crushed
2 tablespoons
  vegetable oil,
  divided
1 pound boneless
  veal cutlet, cut
  into thin strips
2 tablespoons dry
  white wine
12-ounce jar
  Heinz HomeStyle
  chicken gravy
¼ cup sour cream
Hot cooked
  spaghetti or
  linguine

In large skillet, sauté first 8 ingredients in 1 tablespoon oil; remove. Add remaining tablespoon oil. Quickly brown veal in 2 batches; remove.

Add wine; heat. Stir in gravy and sour cream. Return veal and vegetables to skillet; heat slowly.

Serve over spaghetti.

Microwave Directions: Eliminate oil. Reduce pepper to ⅛ teaspoon. In 4-cup glass measure, combine gravy, sour cream, wine, basil, salt, pepper, and oregano; cover with waxed paper. Microwave on high 4 minutes, stirring once. Place veal in 2-quart casserole; cover with waxed paper. Microwave on high 3 to 4 minutes, stirring once. Remove veal from casserole; discard juices. Place carrots in same casserole; cover with lid or vented plastic wrap. Microwave high 2 minutes. Stir in mushrooms, zucchini, and onions; cover. Microwave high 4 minutes, stirring once; drain. Stir in veal and gravy mixture; microwave at high 4 minutes or until hot. Serve over spaghetti. Recipe tested in a 650-watt microwave oven.

Chicken and Turkey Delights

APPLE CURRY CHICKEN

Makes 6 servings

1 package
   Adolph's®
   Marinade in
   Minutes,
   chicken
   flavor
1½ cups apple
   juice
1½ pounds
   boneless
   chicken
   breast, cut
   into 1-inch
   cubes
2 tablespoons
   vegetable oil
1 medium
   onion,
   thinly sliced

1 red bell pepper,
   diced
2 tart apples,
   peeled, cored,
   and diced
¾ cup thinly sliced
   celery
1 tablespoon curry
   powder
1 tablespoon quick-
   mixing flour
½ cup light cream
   Salt to taste
   Hot, cooked rice
½ cup unsalted
   cashew nuts

42

In a shallow bowl, thoroughly combine contents of marinade package with 1 cup apple juice. Place chicken in marinade; pierce deeply with a fork. Marinate 15 minutes.

Remove chicken from marinade; drain thoroughly. In a large skillet, thoroughly cook chicken in 1 tablespoon hot oil. Remove and set aside.

In same skillet, sauté onion, pepper, apples, celery, and curry powder in remaining vegetable oil until tender. Return chicken to skillet.

Add remaining ½ cup apple juice combined with flour to skillet. Stir until thickened. Add cream and salt.

Serve over rice; garnish with cashew nuts.

TOMATO BASIL CHICKEN

Makes 2 servings

½ cup Kretschmer® original or honey crunch wheat germ
1 teaspoon dried basil or 1 tablespoon chopped fresh basil
¼ teaspoon garlic powder
¼ teaspoon black pepper

1 split, boned and skinned chicken breast, pounded ⅛-inch thick
8-ounce can no-salt-added tomato sauce
¼ cup water
¼ cup shredded part-skim mozzarella cheese

Combine first 4 ingredients. Moisten chicken with water; coat with wheat germ mixture, patting on lightly. Repeat procedure; reserve any remaining wheat germ mixture.

Lightly spray 10-inch skillet with no-stick cooking spray. Cook chicken over medium heat 3 minutes per side, or until browned.

Remove chicken from skillet; add tomato sauce, water, and remaining wheat germ mixture. Bring to a boil, stirring occasionally. Return chicken to skillet; spoon sauce over chicken. Sprinkle with cheese. Cover; reduce heat to low until cheese is slightly melted.

Garnish with fresh basil leaves, if desired.

POLYNESIAN CHICKEN

Makes 4 servings

4 skinless boneless chicken breast halves (about 1 pound)
1 medium green pepper, cut into 1-inch chunks
2 tablespoons butter or margarine
¼ teaspoon salt
Dash pepper
two 8-ounce cans pineapple chunks
½ cup water
⅓ cup Heinz apple cider or distilled white vinegar
2 tablespoons brown sugar
2 tablespoons soy sauce
1 teaspoon ginger
2½ tablespoons cornstarch
2½ tablespoons water
Hot cooked rice
Toasted slivered almonds

Cut chicken into strips about 2 inches long. In large skillet, sauté chicken and green pepper in butter just until chicken changes color. Season with salt and pepper.

Stir in pineapple, (including liquid) and next 5 ingredients. Cover; simmer 10 to 12 minutes or until chicken is cooked.

Combine cornstarch and 2½ tablespoons water; stir into chicken mixture. Cook until sauce is thickened, stirring constantly.

Serve over rice; garnish with almonds.

PERFECTLY SIMPLE ROAST CHICKEN

Makes 4 to 6 servings

1 tablespoon flour	2 stalks celery, sliced
1 large (14 by 20-inch) Reynolds oven cooking bag	5–7 pound roasting chicken
	Paprika
1 medium onion, sliced	Salt and pepper

Preheat oven to 350° F.

Shake flour in oven cooking bag; place in 9 by 13 by 2-inch baking pan. Place half the onion and celery in bag.

Rinse chicken; pat dry. Sprinkle cavity of chicken with seasonings; place remaining vegetables inside cavity. Sprinkle outside of chicken with seasonings.

Place chicken in bag on top of vegetables. Close bag with nylon tie; cut six ½-inch slits in top. (If chicken has a pop up thermometer, cut a slit over it.) Bake 1¼ to 1½ hours or until chicken is tender.

Roast Chicken Dinner

Place cooking bag in 10 by 14 by 2-inch roasting pan. Substitute 2 onions, quartered; 2 baking potatoes, cut in ½-inch cubes; and 4 carrots, quartered, for sliced celery and sliced onion. Arrange vegetables in bag around chicken; do not place vegetables inside chicken cavity. Sprinkle chicken and vegetables with thyme or basil leaves, salt and pepper. Bake as directed. Remove chicken from bag. Stir vegetables; serve with chicken.

TANGY CHICKEN WITH TOMATOES

Makes 5 to 6 servings

1 medium onion, sliced
2 cloves garlic, minced
1 teaspoon dried rosemary, crushed
½ teaspoon dried basil, crushed
½ teaspoon dried thyme, crushed
2 tablespoons vegetable oil
16-ounce can tomatoes, drained, cut into bite-sized pieces
¾ cup Heinz tomato ketchup
¼–⅓ cup Heinz apple cider vinegar
1 tablespoon brown sugar
½ teaspoon salt
Dash pepper
2½–3 pounds broiler-fryer pieces, skinned
Cornstarch-water mixture
Hot cooked noodles

In Dutch oven or large skillet, sauté onion, garlic, and herbs in oil until onion is tender-crisp.

Stir in tomatoes and next 5 ingredients.

Add chicken. Bring to a boil; reduce heat and simmer, covered, 45 to 50 minutes or until chicken is tender. Remove chicken.

To thicken sauce, gradually stir in mixture of equal parts cornstarch and water, simmering until thickened.

Serve chicken and sauce with noodles.

BARBECUED CHICKEN OR RIBS

Makes 4 to 6 servings

2½ to 3-pound broiler-fryer chicken, cut up
1 cup ketchup
½ cup Grandma's® molasses (Gold Label)
¼ cup cider vinegar
¼ cup Dijon mustard

2 tablespoons Worcestershire sauce
1 teaspoon garlic powder
1 teaspoon hickory flavor liquid smoke
¼ teaspoon cayenne pepper
¼ teaspoon hot pepper sauce

In 8 by 12-inch (2-quart) microwave-safe baking dish, arrange chicken pieces with thickest portions to outside. In small bowl, combine all other ingredients; set aside.

Prepare barbecue grill. Cover chicken with waxed paper. Microwave on 100 percent (high) for 10 minutes. Immediately place chicken on grill over medium heat. Brush with sauce. Cook 20 to 25 minutes or until no longer pink, turning once and brushing frequently with sauce.

CHICKEN FAJITAS

Makes 6 servings

1 package
   Adolph's®
   Marinade in
   Minutes,
   Mexican
   grill flavor
⅓ cup water
⅓ cup lime juice
1½ pounds boneless
   chicken breast,
   sliced into
   thin strips
1 tablespoon
   vegetable oil
4-ounce can
   chopped
   green chilis,
   drained

2¼-ounce can sliced
   ripe olives,
   drained
1 teaspoon chili
   powder
½ teaspoon cumin
½ cup sliced
   scallions
6 large flour
   tortillas,
   warmed
Mexican salsa
Shredded
   Cheddar
   cheese
Sour cream
Chopped
   avocados

In a shallow bowl, thoroughly combine contents of marinade package with water and lime juice. Place chicken in marinade; pierce deeply with a fork. Marinate 15 minutes.

Remove chicken from marinade; drain thoroughly. In a large skillet, thoroughly cook chicken in hot oil. Add chilis, olives, chili powder, cumin, and scallions; heat through.

Serve in tortillas with salsa, cheese, sour cream, and avocado.

CHICKEN WITH RED GRAPES

Makes 6 servings

2 tablespoons olive oil	⅛ teaspoon freshly ground pepper
1 large red onion, thinly sliced	⅛ teaspoon crushed rosemary
6 chicken breast halves, boned and skinned	1 cup seedless red grapes
⅔ cup Welch's red grape juice	⅔ cup heavy cream
	1 tablespoon paprika

Heat oil in a large skillet over medium-high heat. Sauté onion in oil for 1 minute. Add chicken; sauté on both sides until golden brown.

Reduce heat to medium; pour in red grape juice. Cover and cook 5 minutes. Add pepper, rosemary, grapes, and heavy cream; continue cooking until heated through, about 5 minutes.

Transfer chicken and grapes to heated serving platter using a slotted spoon. Continue cooking sauce until reduced by half. Pour sauce around chicken; sprinkle chicken with paprika.

CHICKEN INDIENNE

Makes 6 to 8 servings

1¾ cups Welch's white grape juice

1½–2 tablespoons curry powder

2 egg yolks

6 pounds chicken parts

Salt and pepper to taste

2 cups crushed cornflakes (6 cups whole flakes)

1 cup flaked coconut

1 tablespoon grated orange peel

2 teaspoons cornstarch

In a large shallow baking dish (use two if necessary), combine white grape juice, curry powder, and egg yolks. Lightly, season chicken with salt and pepper and add to baking dish. Cover and marinate in the refrigerator several hours or overnight, turning chicken occasionally.

Preheat oven to 375° F. Drain chicken, reserving marinade. On plate, combine cornflakes, coconut, and orange peel. Coat chicken with cornflake mixture; arrange on rack in shallow baking pan. Sprinkle with any remaining cornflakes mixture. Bake 1 hour or until chicken is tender.

Meanwhile, place reserved marinade in saucepan. Stir in cornstarch until smooth. Stir over low heat until thickened.

Serve sauce with chicken. If desired, serve with chutney. Other nice accompaniments include brown rice, chopped cucumber and tomatoes marinated in yogurt (an Indian dish called *raita*), and green peas.

STUFFED CHICKEN BREASTS

Makes 6 servings

6 tablespoons
butter, divided

¼ cup onion,
finely chopped

½ pound
mushrooms,
finely chopped

1 cup Lea &
Perrins white
wine
Worcestershire
sauce, divided

3 whole chicken
breasts, skinned,
boned, and
halved

1 each red, yellow,
and green bell
pepper, in strips

2 tablespoons
vegetable oil

Parsley for garnish

Preheat oven to 350° F.

In a skillet, over medium heat, melt 2 tablespoons butter. Add onions; sauté until golden. Add mushrooms and ½ cup Worcestershire sauce. Sauté on high heat until liquid has evaporated and mixture is dry.

Place chicken in ovenproof dish. Tuck about 2 tablespoons mushroom mixture under the filet of each chicken breast. Melt remaining butter and add the remaining Worcestershire sauce and pour over chicken. Bake for 35 minutes, or until chicken is tender and lightly brown, basting occasionally.

Sauté pepper strips in oil and serve with the chicken. Garnish with minced parsley.

CHICKEN DIJON

Makes 2 servings

2 chicken breast portions, boneless, about 4 ounces each
½ teaspoon salt
¼ teaspoon pepper
2 tablespoons butter

¼ cup sour cream
2 tablespoons Lea & Perrins Worcestershire sauce
1½ tablespoons Dijon mustard
2 teaspoons chopped chives (optional)

Season chicken breast portions lightly with salt and pepper. Heat butter in skillet and brown chicken about 5 minutes on each side, pressing flat with spatula.

While chicken browns, combine sour cream, Worcestershire sauce and mustard. Spoon sauce over chicken portions and warm through, a minute or two.

Sprinkle with chopped chives, if desired, and serve.

SPICY BARBECUE DRUMSTICKS

Makes 3 to 4 servings

1 tablespoon flour
1 regular (10 by 16-inch) Reynolds oven cooking bag
1 cup barbecue sauce
1 tablespoon chili powder

1 tablespoon mustard
¼ teaspoon garlic powder
6–8 chicken drumsticks

Preheat oven to 350° F.

Shake flour in cooking bag; place in 9 by 13 by 2-inch baking pan. Add barbecue sauce, chili powder, mustard, and garlic powder to bag. Squeeze bag to blend ingredients.

Place chicken in bag. Turn bag to coat chicken with sauce. Arrange chicken in an even layer. Close bag with nylon tie; cut six ½-inch slits in top. Bake 40 minutes or until chicken is tender.

Note: Sauce will cause the top of the bag to darken in color. This is a normal reaction and does not indicate burning.

ITALIAN CHICKEN

Makes 4 servings

2 tablespoons
flour

1 regular (10 by
16-inch)
Reynolds
oven cooking
bag

15¼-ounce jar
spaghetti
sauce with
mushrooms

¼ cup water

4 skinless,
boneless chicken
breast halves

1 small onion, thinly
sliced

1 small green
pepper, cut into
strips

7-ounce package
spaghetti,
cooked and
drained

Grated Parmesan
cheese

Preheat oven to 350° F.

Shake flour in cooking bag; place in 9 by 13 by 2-inch baking pan. Add spaghetti sauce and water to bag. Squeeze bag to blend ingredients. Place chicken breasts in bag. Turn bag to coat chicken with sauce. Arrange chicken in an even layer. Place onion and green pepper in bag on top of chicken. Close bag with nylon tie; cut six ½-inch slits in top.

Bake 35 minutes or until chicken is tender.

Serve chicken and sauce over hot cooked spaghetti. Sprinkle with Parmesan cheese.

Note: Sauce will cause the top of the bag to darken in color. This is a normal reaction and does not indicate burning.

CHICKEN AND RICE ESPAÑOL

Makes 4 servings

2 to 2½ pounds broiler fryer pieces, skinned
1 tablespoon vegetable oil
1 medium onion, chopped
1–2 cloves garlic, minced
¾ cup uncooked white rice
⅓ cup coarsely chopped red bell pepper

1½ cups water
½ cup Heinz tomato ketchup
1 teaspoon salt
¼ teaspoon pepper
¼ cup chopped pimiento-stuffed olives
1 tablespoon drained capers

In large skillet, brown chicken in oil; remove.

In same skillet, sauté onion, garlic, rice, and red bell pepper until rice is golden brown. Stir in water, ketchup, salt, and pepper.

Return chicken to skillet. Cover; simmer 30 minutes, spooning rice and liquid over chicken occasionally. (Dark meat may require an additional 5 minutes cooking time.) Remove chicken; stir olives and capers into rice.

SPICY CHICKEN SAUTÉ

Makes 4 servings

⅓ cup Heinz
    tomato
    ketchup
¼ cup apple
    juice
1½ teaspoons
    curry
    powder
½ teaspoon salt
⅛ teaspoon
    pepper
⅛ teaspoon dried
    thyme leaves,
    crushed
1 medium green
    pepper, cut
    into thin
    strips

1 medium red bell
    pepper, cut into
    thin strips
1 medium onion,
    cut into eighths
1 clove garlic,
    minced
2 tablespoons
    vegetable oil,
    divided
4 skinless boneless
    chicken breast
    halves (about 1
    pound), cut into
    ½-inch strips
⅓ cup raisins,
    plumped
¼ cup peanuts

Combine first 6 ingredients; set aside.

In large skillet, sauté green pepper and next 3 ingredients in 1 tablespoon oil until tender-crisp; remove.

Heat remaining oil in skillet; sauté chicken 2 to 3 minutes or until chicken changes color. Stir in ketchup mixture and raisins. Cook, stirring constantly, 2 to 3 minutes or until chicken is cooked and sauce is hot and bubbly. Return vegetables to skillet; stir to coat. Heat thoroughly.

Garnish with peanuts.

CHILI CON QUESO PIE

Makes 6 servings

2 cups diced
   cooked
   chicken
12-ounce jar
   mild,
   medium, or
   hot thick and
   chunky salsa
2 cups water

½ cup regular,
   Instant or
   Quick Cream of
   Wheat® cereal
2 tablespoons sliced
   scallions
⅛ teaspoon ground
   black pepper
Sour cream
   (optional)

Preheat oven to 375° F.

In 8 by 8 by 2-inch baking pan, mix chicken and salsa, set aside.

In large saucepan, over high heat, heat water to a boil; slowly sprinkle in cereal, stirring constantly. Return mixture to a boil; reduce heat. Cook and stir until thickened, about 2 to 3 minutes; remove from heat.

Stir in 1 tablespoon scallions and pepper; spoon cereal mixture over chicken in pan.

Bake for 15 minutes or until bubbling around edges of pan and browned on top. Serve immediately topped with remaining scallions and sour cream if desired.

CHICKEN BREASTS PROVOLONE

Makes 4 servings

2 tablespoons all-
  purpose flour
1 teaspoon
  tarragon
½ teaspoon salt
¼ teaspoon white
  pepper
4 skinned, boned
  chicken
  breast halves
2 tablespoons
  butter

4 slices (2 ounces)
  boiled ham
2 teaspoons flour
⅓ cup dry white
  wine
⅔ cup undiluted
  Carnation®
  evaporated
  milk
1 cup (4 ounces)
  shredded
  provolone
  cheese

Combine 2 tablespoons flour, tarragon, salt, and pepper in plastic bag; add chicken. Shake well to coat.

Melt butter in medium skillet. Sauté chicken over medium heat until golden and cooked through. Remove to heated platter.

Cut ham into strips; cook 2 to 3 minutes in same skillet. Place over chicken; keep warm.

Stir 2 teaspoons flour into drippings in skillet; blend well. Stir in wine with wire whisk; gradually stir in evaporated milk. Cook over medium heat until mixture just comes to a boil and thickens. Stir in cheese until melted.

Serve immediately with chicken, ham, and wild rice, if desired.

CLASSIC HERB CHICKEN

Makes 4 servings

1 cup Kretschmer® wheat germ	¼ teaspoon salt (optional)
1 tablespoon Italian seasoning	¼ teaspoon black pepper
2 teaspoons dried parsley	½ cup water
	1 egg white
2 teaspoons dried minced onion	2 split and skinned chicken breasts or one 2½ to 3 pound chicken, cut up and skinned
1 teaspoon garlic powder	

Preheat oven to 400° F.

Combine wheat germ and seasonings; set aside.

Combine water and egg white. Dip chicken into egg white mixture, and then into wheat germ mixture, coating chicken thoroughly.

Place in 9 by 13 by 2-inch baking pan; spray each chicken breast for about 3 seconds with no-stick cooking spray. Bake 45 minutes or until tender and golden brown.

SOUTHWEST CHICKEN BURGERS

Makes 6 burgers

8-ounce carton
plain low-fat
yogurt
1 tablespoon finely
chopped
fresh parsley
or 1 teaspoon
dried parsley
1 teaspoon chili
powder
½ teaspoon ground
cumin

¼ teaspoon cayenne
pepper
2 cups chopped
cooked chicken
⅔ cup Kretschmer®
wheat germ
2 egg whites,
slightly beaten
6 whole wheat
hamburger
buns

Lightly spray rack of broiler pan with no-stick cooking spray. Combine first 5 ingredients.

In separate bowl, combine chicken, wheat germ, egg whites, and ½ cup prepared yogurt sauce; mix well.

Shape into 6 patties. Place on prepared broiler rack. Broil 5 minutes; turn. Continue broiling 5 to 7 minutes or until golden brown. Top each burger with remaining yogurt sauce. Serve on buns with lettuce and tomato, if desired.

WARM GINGER ALMOND CHICKEN SALAD

Makes 4 servings

¼ cup oil
¼ cup cider
  vinegar
⅓ cup
  Grandma's®
  molasses
  (Gold Label)
1 teaspoon finely
  chopped
  fresh ginger or
  ½ teaspoon
  ginger
1 teaspoon soy
  sauce
½ teaspoon salt
  Dash hot
  pepper sauce

1 pound chicken
  breasts,
  skinned, boned,
  cut into thin
  strips
4 cups torn mixed
  greens
1 cup (2 medium)
  shredded
  carrots
¼ cup chopped
  green onions
1 tablespoon
  cornstarch
2 tablespoons water
¼ cup sliced
  almonds, toasted

In medium bowl, combine oil, vinegar, molasses, ginger, soy sauce, pepper, salt, and pepper sauce. Add chicken strips; blend well. Cover; refrigerate 1 to 2 hours.

In serving bowl, combine greens, carrots and green onions. Refrigerate.

In large skillet, place chicken and marinade. Bring to a boil, cooking and stirring until chicken is no longer pink, about 3 to 5 minutes. In small bowl, combine cornstarch and water; blend well.

Stir into chicken mixture; cook until mixture thickens, stirring constantly. Spoon hot chicken mixture over vegetables; toss to combine. Sprinkle with almonds. Serve immediately.

SWEET AND SOUR CHICKEN SALAD

Makes 4 servings

½ cup Heinz chili
　　sauce
⅓ cup apple juice
1 tablespoon
　　Heinz distilled
　　white vinegar
2 teaspoons
　　cornstarch
2 teaspoons sugar
2 cups cubed
　　cooked
　　chicken
　　8-ounce can
　　sliced water
　　chestnuts,
　　drained

1 small zucchini,
　　halved
　　lengthwise,
　　sliced (about 1
　　cup)
1 medium red
　　apple, cut into
　　chunks
¾ cup sliced celery
　　Leaf lettuce
1 cup chow mein
　　noodles

Combine first 5 ingredients in 1-quart saucepan. Bring to boiling over medium heat, stirring constantly. Boil 1 minute or until thickened and clear; cool slightly.

In medium bowl, combine chicken, water chestnuts, zucchini, apple, and celery. Pour warm dressing over chicken mixture; mix well.

Serve on lettuce. Sprinkle with chow mein noodles.

GRILLED CHICKEN SALAD VINAIGRETTE

Makes 6 to 8 servings

1 package Adolph's® Marinade in Minutes, lemon-pepper flavor
½ cup wine vinegar
¼ cup water
2 pounds boneless chicken breasts
1 cup thinly sliced celery
1 medium onion, sliced
7-ounce jar roasted peppers, drained and sliced
6-ounce jar marinated artichoke hearts, drained and sliced
2¼-ounce can sliced ripe olives, drained
⅓ cup olive oil
3 tablespoons wine vinegar
1 teaspoon Dijon mustard
Salt to taste
Pepper to taste
Leaf lettuce

Preheat grill or broiler.

In a medium bowl, thoroughly combine contents of marinade package with ½ cup vinegar and ¼ cup water. Place chicken in marinade; pierce deeply with a fork. Marinate 15 minutes, turning chicken occasionally. Remove chicken from marinade. Grill or broil chicken 5 to 6 inches from heat, 5 to 7 minutes per side or until thoroughly cooked. Thinly slice chicken; let cool.

Combine sliced chicken with celery, onion, roasted peppers, artichoke hearts, olives, olive oil, vinegar, mustard, salt, and pepper. Stir to combine thoroughly. Serve chilled over leaf lettuce.

TURKEY CREOLE

Makes 4 to 6 servings

1¼ pounds Shady Brook Farms® fresh turkey thighs, cut into ½-inch pieces

3 tablespoons hot cooking oil, divided

1½ cups chopped peeled onion

1½ cups coarsely chopped green pepper

1 cup thinly sliced celery

2 teaspoons minced peeled garlic

28-ounce can Italian-style tomatoes, undrained

10-ounce package frozen sliced okra, thawed, or 8 to 12 ounces thinly sliced fresh okra

2 bay leaves, crumbled

1 teaspoon dried or 1 tablespoon minced fresh oregano

¼ teaspoon cayenne pepper

2–3 cups hot cooked rice

2 tablespoons minced parsley

In a Dutch oven or large heavy saucepan, sauté turkey in 1 tablespoon oil over moderate heat for 5 minutes, stirring frequently. Reduce heat and continue cooking for 10 minutes. Drain oil from turkey.

In a small heavy skillet, sauté onion, green pepper, celery, and garlic in remaining 2 tablespoons of oil, stirring frequently, over moderate heat until tender, about 5 minutes. Stir onion mixture and remaining ingredients, except rice and parsley, into turkey. Simmer, uncovered, for 20 to 25 minutes, stirring occasionally. (Add 5 to 10 minutes cooking time if using fresh okra.) Serve over rice and garnish with minced parsley.

TURKEY FLORENTINE

Makes 4 servings

10-ounce package frozen chopped spinach

4 large slices cooked turkey (or 2 cups cubed cooked turkey)

1 cup Ricotta cheese

½ cup grated Parmesan cheese

6 green onions, thinly sliced

1 egg yolk

1 teaspoon dried basil, divided

¼ teaspoon pepper, divided

1 clove garlic, minced

1 teaspoon vegetable oil

1 small tomato, peeled, chopped (about ½ cup)

12-ounce jar Heinz HomeStyle turkey gravy

3 tablespoons plain yogurt or sour cream

Preheat oven to 375° F.

Cook spinach following package directions; place in colander and press out excess moisture.

Arrange turkey in 1½-quart oblong baking dish. Combine spinach, cheeses, onions, egg yolk, ½ teaspoon basil, and ⅛ teaspoon pepper. Place ¼ of spinach mixture on each turkey slice; spread to edges. Bake for 25 to 30 minutes or until thoroughly heated.

Meanwhile, for sauce, sauté garlic in oil. Add tomato, remaining ½ teaspoon basil, and ⅛ teaspoon pepper. Cook, uncovered, over low heat 4 to 5 minutes. Stir in gravy and yogurt. Heat. *Do not boil.* Spoon small amount of sauce on each of 4 serving plates. Place turkey on top of sauce, then spoon additional sauce over turkey.

TURKEY SAUSAGE AND VEGETABLE KABOBS

Makes 4 servings

6 tablespoons olive oil

2 tablespoons lemon juice

2 cloves garlic, minced

2 tablespoons fresh parsley, chopped

1 teaspoon grated lemon peel

½ teaspoon salt

¼ teaspoon ground pepper

6 links (about 1 pound) Shady Brook Farms® sweet or hot Italian turkey sausage, cut diagonally into 1½-inch pieces

6 ounces zucchini, cut into ½-inch slices

6 ounces yellow squash, cut into ½-inch slices

1 large red bell pepper, seeded and cut into 1½-inch pieces

Combine oil, lemon juice, garlic, parsley, lemon peel, salt, and pepper in a medium bowl. Add sausage to marinade, stirring to coat; refrigerate several hours or overnight, turning occasionally.

Prepare charcoal for grilling or heat broiler. Alternate vegetables and sausage on four 10-inch metal skewers. Brush all sides with marinade.

Grill or broil kabobs four inches from source of heat, turning once, until sausage is no longer pink in the center. Cook about 15 to 20 minutes.

Serve immediately.

GRILLED TARRAGON TURKEY TENDERLOINS

Makes 4 servings

6 tablespoons
   olive oil
2 tablespoons red
   wine vinegar
1 tablespoon
   Dijon mustard
1 large clove
   garlic, minced
¼ cup fresh
   tarragon or 2
   teaspoons
   dried tarragon,
   crumbled

½ teaspoon salt
¼ teaspoon ground
   pepper
2 Shady Brook
   Farms® turkey
   tenderloins
   (about ¾ pound
   each)

Whisk oil, vinegar, mustard, garlic, tarragon, salt, and pepper in small bowl. Pour over tenderloins and marinate several hours or overnight, turning occasionally.

Prepare charcoal for grilling or heat broiler. Grill or broil tenderloins, turning once, until turkey is no longer pink in the center. Cook 20 to 25 minutes; let cool slightly; cut into ½-inch medallions.

Serve immediately.

TURKEY WITH CHILI CRANBERRY SAUCE

Makes 4 servings

1 pound ground turkey
⅓ cup dry bread crumbs
¼ cup finely chopped onion
¼ cup Heinz chili sauce
1 egg, slightly beaten
½ teaspoon salt
¼ teaspoon pepper
1 tablespoon vegetable oil
⅔ cup whole berry cranberry sauce
⅓ cup Heinz chili sauce
2 tablespoons water
⅛ teaspoon cinnamon

Combine first 7 ingredients. Shape into 4 patties, about ½-inch thick. Slowly sauté patties in oil, about 7 minutes per side or until cooked.

Meanwhile, for sauce, combine cranberry sauce and next 3 ingredients in small saucepan. Simmer, uncovered, 5 minutes. Spoon sauce over patties.

Note: To broil, eliminate oil. Broil patties about 7 inches from heat source, 7 minutes per side or until cooked.

SWEET AND SOUR TURKEY WING PORTIONS OR DRUMETTES

Makes 4 to 6 servings

3½ pounds Shady Brook Farms® fresh turkey wing portions or 3½ pounds fresh turkey wing drumettes

1–2 tablespoons butter or margarine, at room temperature

20-ounce can pineapple tidbits (reserve juice)

Water

1 cup sugar

2 tablespoons cornstarch

3¼ cup cider vinegar

1 tablespoon soy sauce

⅛–¼ teaspoon ginger

⅛ teaspoon white pepper

1 tablespoon chopped pimento, drained

½ cup sliced green onions, diagonally cut into 1-inch pieces

½ medium green pepper, cored, seeded, and thinly sliced lengthwise

Preheat oven to 350° F.

Arrange turkey pieces in an ungreased 9 by 9 by 2-inch baking pan; dot turkey with butter. Bake, loosely covered with aluminum foil, shiny side turned in, for 1 hour.

Drain pineapple, pouring syrup into a 2-cup measure; add enough water so mixture equals 1¼ cups. In a heavy saucepan, combine reserved pineapple juice, sugar, cornstarch, vinegar, soy sauce, ginger, and pepper, stirring constantly; bring to a boil.

Remove from heat; blend in drained pineapple and pimento. Spoon over turkey and continue baking, uncovered, for 1 hour or until turkey is fork tender.

Add onions and green pepper during last 10 to 15 minutes of baking.

STUFFED TURKEY DRUMSTICKS

Makes 4 to 6 servings

4–6 pounds Shady Brook Farms® fresh turkey drumsticks	8 ounces Canadian-style bacon, minced
Salt and pepper to taste	¼ cup fine bread crumbs
4 large mushrooms, minced	¼ cup minced parsley
	⅛–¼ teaspoon poultry seasoning

Preheat oven to 350° F.

With a sharp knife, make one slit lengthwise in each drumstick. Leaving outside skin intact, push meat back from bone. With knife, remove bone and cartilage. Sprinkle inside of each boned drumstick lightly with salt and pepper.

In a small bowl, combine mushrooms, Canadian bacon, bread crumbs, parsley, and poultry seasoning; mix well. Evenly spoon mixture into seasoned pocket of each drumstick. Roll and close drumstick meat over stuffing, securing tightly with skewers, wooden picks, or heavy string. Arrange stuffed drumsticks in a greased 9 by 13 by 2-inch baking pan. Bake, loosely covered, for 45 to 50 minutes. Uncover and continue baking until drumsticks are lightly browned and fork tender, about 25 to 30 minutes.

To serve, cut into ½-inch thick slices. Serve warm or chilled.

ITALIAN TURKEY BURGER

Makes 4 servings

1 pound Shady Brook Farms® ground turkey	4 slices red onion, cut ½-inch thick
1 tablespoon ground oregano	4 teaspoons olive oil
1 teaspoon garlic powder	4 hamburger rolls, split and lightly toasted, if desired
¼ teaspoon ground pepper	2 roasted red peppers, halved
Salt to taste	2 tablespoons grated Parmesan cheese

Prepare charcoal for grilling or heat broiler.

Using your hands, gently mix ground turkey with oregano, garlic powder, and pepper in a small mixing bowl. Gently shape into 4 patties, about 1-inch thick.

Grill patties and onion or broil approximately 4 inches from source of heat. Cook patties about 14 to 15 minutes, until done in the center, turning once. Brush onion with half the oil and cook, turning once, brushing second side with remaining oil until brown, about 7 to 10 minutes.

Place turkey burger on each roll. Top each with red pepper, onion, and Parmesan cheese, divided evenly.

Serve at once.

STARBURST TURKEY SALAD

Makes 8 servings

2½-pounds package Shady Brook Farms® boneless turkey breast, cooked, skin removed and diced into ½-inch cubes
1 cup mayonnaise
½ cup sour cream
4 stalks celery, diced
2 large tomatoes, seeded and diced

⅔ cup chopped toasted pecans
1½ teaspoons dried tarragon
½ teaspoon each ground pepper and salt
8 pita breads
3 heads Bibb lettuce
2 medium yellow peppers, seeded and julienned

In a large bowl, combine turkey, mayonnaise, sour cream, celery, tomato, pecans, tarragon, salt, and pepper; mix well. Cut an X in the top of each pita. Fold back cut sections and line pita with lettuce leaves and then fill with turkey salad. Garnish with yellow pepper strips.

Vegetables

STIR-FRIED BROCCOLI AND WATER CHESTNUTS

Makes 4 servings

1 pound bunch broccoli	2 teaspoons salt
¼ cup peanut or vegetable oil	½ teaspoon sugar
8-ounce can water chestnuts, drained and sliced	¼ cup water
	½ teaspoon sesame oil (optional)

Cut broccoli into small florets. With sharp knife, remove coarse green sections from stems; slice stems crosswise into thin slices.

In Farberware® electric wok, add oil. Set heat control dial at 250° F. When light goes out, add broccoli florets and stems, water chestnuts, salt, sugar, and water. Cover. Steam about 5 minutes. Remove cover and stir occasionally until broccoli is tender and crisp. Stir in sesame oil.

Serve immediately.

GLAZED SWEET POTATOES

Makes 3 to 4 servings

1-pound can sweet
    potatoes or
    yams
3 tablespoons
    butter or
    margarine

½ cup firmly packed
    brown sugar
⅓ cup Heinz tomato
    ketchup
2 tablespoons water

Preheat oven to 350° F. Arrange sweet potatoes in greased shallow baking dish.

In saucepan, combine remaining ingredients; simmer 5 minutes. Pour sauce over sweet potatoes; bake 30 minutes, basting occasionally.

POTATO SALAD VINAIGRETTE

Makes 6 to 8 servings

2 pounds new
    potatoes
    (about
    6 medium)
6 slices bacon,
    cooked,
    crumbled
2 hard-cooked
    eggs,
    chopped
2 tablespoons
    chopped
    fresh parsley

½ cup thinly sliced
    green onions
⅓ cup vegetable oil
¼ cup Heinz
    distilled white
    or apple cider
    vinegar
2 teaspoons Dijon
    mustard
½ teaspoon salt
¼ teaspoon pepper

Cook potatoes in boiling water until just tender; cool. Peel potatoes and cut into small cubes, about 4 cups. In medium bowl, combine potatoes and next 4 ingredients.

For dressing, combine oil and remaining ingredients in jar; cover and shake vigorously. Pour dressing over potato mixture; toss gently.

SAVORY MASHED POTATO CAKES

Makes 6 servings

4 cups slightly
    firm mashed
    potatoes
1 egg yolk
½ cup Kretschmer®
    wheat germ,
    divided
1 tablespoon
    parsley flakes

½ teaspoon instant
    onion powder
½ teaspoon salt
¼ teaspoon pepper
2–3 tablespoons
    cooking oil

Beat egg yolk into potatoes with fork. Stir in ¼ cup wheat germ, parsley flakes, onion powder, salt, and pepper. Shape into patties. Roll in additional wheat germ.

Brown in oil in skillet over low heat about 5 minutes on each side.

NEW POTATO SALAD

Makes 6 servings

2 pounds new
    potatoes
1 red onion,
    thinly sliced
½ cup vegetable
    oil

½ cup Lea &
    Perrins white
    wine
    Worcestershire
    sauce
1 tablespoon
    chopped parsley

Cook the potatoes in boiling salted water until just tender. Drain, peel, and cut into ¼-inch slices.

In a bowl, place potato slices and onion slices. Combine oil, Worcestershire sauce, and parsley and pour over salad. Toss gently until most of the liquid is absorbed.

Serve warm.

CRUNCHY GREEN BEAN CASSEROLE

Makes 2 servings

1 tablespoon
    margarine
¼ cup
    Kretschmer®
    wheat germ
2 tablespoons
    oats (quick or
    old-
    fashioned,
    uncooked)
2 teaspoons
    Italian
    seasoning

¼ teaspoon garlic
    powder
1 cup green beans,
    cut into 1½-
    inch pieces
¾ cup sliced
    mushrooms
½ cup chopped
    onion
½ cup plain low-fat
    yogurt
2 teaspoons
    cornstarch

In 8- or 9-inch glass pie plate or small microwaveable casserole, microwave margarine on high 15 to 30 seconds or until melted.

Add wheat germ, oats, Italian seasoning, and garlic powder; mix well. Microwave on high 2 to 3 minutes or until golden brown, stirring after each minute. Remove mixture from pie plate; set aside.

In same pie plate, combine beans, mushrooms, and onion. Microwave on high 3 to 4 minutes, stirring after 2 minutes.

Stir in combined yogurt and cornstarch, coating vegetables thoroughly. Microwave on high 1½ to 2½ minutes or until sauce is slightly thickened; stir.

Sprinkle with reserved wheat germ mixture before serving.

Note: 2 cups of frozen, unthawed vegetable mixture of green beans, broccoli, mushrooms, and onion may be substituted for fresh vegetables. Drain vegetables well before adding yogurt mixture.

BROILED STUFFED MUSHROOMS

Makes 4 servings

2 tablespoons butter or margarine
24 large mushrooms, stems removed and chopped
¼ cup chopped onion
1½ cups flavored bread crumbs
1 cup finely chopped cooked ham
¼ cup heavy cream
1½ teaspoons mustard
½ teaspoon pepper
2 tablespoons butter or margarine, melted

Melt 2 tablespoons of butter in small skillet. Add chopped mushroom stems and onion. Sauté 4 to 5 minutes. Remove mixture to bowl.

Add remaining ingredients except 2 tablespoons melted butter. Mix well and set aside.

Dip mushroom caps into reserved melted butter. Spoon about 1 to 2 teaspoons of filling into each mushroom cap. Preheat Farberware® smokeless indoor grill with rack in high position. Place stuffed mushrooms on rack with stuffing up. Broil 10 to 15 minutes.

Stuffed mushrooms are also good to serve as a garnish for main dishes, or serve individual mushrooms as appetizers.

GINGERED BROCCOLI

Makes 6 to 8 servings

2 tablespoons
  olive oil
¼ teaspoon hot
  sesame oil
1 large bunch
  broccoli,
  trimmed and
  cut into
  florets
½ red pepper, cut
  into strips

2 tablespoons Lea
  & Perrins
  Worcestershire
  sauce
¼ cup water
1 teaspoon grated
  fresh ginger (or
  ¼ teaspoon dry
  ginger)

In a large skillet, heat olive oil and sesame oil.
Add broccoli florets and red pepper strips and cook
over medium heat, stirring often, for 4 minutes,
until tender and crisp.

Combine Worcestershire sauce, water, and ginger; add to pan and toss to combine. Cover pan and
steam for 2 minutes longer.

Serve hot or at room temperature.

MICROWAVE HERBED CORN-ON-THE-COB

Makes 3 to 4 servings

1 tablespoon flour
1 large (14 by 20-inch) Reynolds oven cooking bag
2 tablespoons grated Parmesan cheese
½ teaspoon rosemary or basil
½ teaspoon salt (optional)
⅛ teaspoon pepper
½ cup water
¼ cup margarine or butter, diced
3–4 medium ears fresh or frozen corn

Shake flour in cooking bag; place in 8 by 12 by 2-inch microwave-safe baking dish. Add cheese, rosemary, salt, pepper, water, and margarine to bag. Squeeze bag to blend ingredients.

Place corn in bag; turn bag to coat corn with sauce. Arrange corn in a single layer. Close bag with nylon tie; cut six ½-inch slits in top of bag. Microwave on high 9 to 14 minutes or until corn is tender, rotating dish once after 5 minutes. Let stand in bag 2 minutes.

Stir sauce; serve over corn.

BROCCOLI-CHEESE SOUFFLÉ

Makes 6 servings

2 cups milk
½ cup regular,
    Instant or
    Quick Cream
    of Wheat®
    cereal
2 cups chopped
    cooked
    broccoli

1 cup shredded
    reduced-fat
    Cheddar cheese
2 eggs, separated
¼ teaspoon ground
    black pepper
¼ teaspoon dry
    mustard

Preheat oven to 400° F.

In large saucepan, over high heat, heat milk to a boil; slowly sprinkle in cereal, stirring constantly. Return mixture to a boil; reduce heat. Cook and stir until thickened, about 2 to 3 minutes. Remove from heat.

Stir in broccoli and cheese until cheese melts; blend in egg yolks, pepper, and mustard. Let cool 10 minutes.

In small bowl, with electric mixer, beat egg whites until stiff peaks form; gently fold into broccoli mixture. Spoon into 1½-quart soufflé or casserole dish. Bake for 30 minutes or until puffed and golden.

Serve immediately.

Pasta and Rice

SIDE DISH MACARONI BAKE

Makes 6 servings

4 ounces elbow macaroni
¼ cup finely chopped onion
1 tablespoon margarine
1½ cups cream-style cottage cheese
1 cup sour cream
1 tablespoon Lea & Perrins Worcestershire sauce
½ teaspoon salt
1 teaspoon hot pepper sauce

Preheat oven to 350° F.

Cook macaroni in boiling water until tender; drain. Sauté onion in margarine until tender. Combine macaroni and onion in large bowl. Stir in cottage cheese, sour cream, Worcestershire sauce, salt, and hot pepper sauce.

Turn into a 6 by 10 by 2-inch baking dish. Bake for 25 to 30 minutes or until hot.

When done, serve from baking dish or place in individual side dishes.

Garnish with paprika or crumbled bacon bits.

TARRAGON TURKEY AND ASPARAGUS LINGUINE

Makes 4 to 6 servings

2½ cups Shady Brook Farms® fresh turkey cut into ½-inch cubes or cubed cooked turkey

6 tablespoons minced peeled onion

6 tablespoons butter or margarine, melted

2 tablespoons flour

1 teaspoon salt

¼ teaspoon pepper or to taste

1 cup milk

12 fresh asparagus spears, cooked and cut into 1-inch pieces

¾ teaspoon dried or 1½ to 2¼ teaspoons minced fresh tarragon

8-ounce package linguine

¾ cup grated Parmesan cheese

In a large heavy saucepan, sauté turkey and onion in butter over moderate heat until turkey is lightly browned and onion is tender. Stir in flour, salt, and pepper; reduce heat and cook for 2 minutes, stirring occasionally. Do not allow mixture to brown. Gradually add milk; cook, stirring constantly, until sauce begins to boil. Cook 1 minute longer. Add asparagus and tarragon, mixing well. Continue to cook, stirring occasionally, until mixture is bubbly hot.

Cook linguine according to package directions; drain. Arrange linguine on a heated platter. Spoon turkey mixture over linguine. Add grated Parmesan cheese and toss lightly.

Serve with additional Parmesan cheese, if desired.

ITALIAN STUFFED PASTA WITH WHEAT GERM

Makes 4 servings

8 manicotti
  tubes
½ cup finely
  chopped
  onion
2 tablespoons
  butter or
  margarine
two 15-ounce cans
  tomato sauce
⅛ teaspoon garlic
  powder
1 pound lean
  ground beef
⅔ cup Kretschmer®
  wheat germ

¼ cup grated
  Parmesan
  cheese
1 teaspoon oregano,
  crushed
½ teaspoon basil,
  crushed
½ teaspoon salt
¼ teaspoon pepper
6 ounces Monterey
  Jack cheese,
  sliced
1 tablespoon
  minced parsley

Preheat oven to 425° F.

Cook manicotti tubes as package directs. Drain.

Sauté onion in butter until tender. Stir in tomato sauce and garlic powder. Set aside.

Brown beef. Remove from heat. Add wheat germ, Parmesan cheese, oregano, basil, salt, pepper, and ¾ cup sauce to beef. Mix well. Fill manicotti tubes with meat mixture. Add remaining meat mixture to sauce. Pour half of sauce into large baking dish. Place stuffed manicotti on sauce in single layer. Top with Monterey Jack cheese. Pour remaining sauce around outside edge. Cover. Bake for 25 minutes until thoroughly heated.

Sprinkle with parsley.

CHEESE LASAGNE

Makes 8 to 10 servings

1 medium onion, chopped	½ teaspoon basil leaves, crushed
3 small cloves garlic, minced	¼ teaspoon crushed red pepper
2 tablespoons cooking oil	8 ounces lasagne noodles
28-ounce can peeled tomatoes	1½ cups (15- to 16-ounce carton) Ricotta cheese
two 6-ounce cans tomato paste	1 pound Mozzarella cheese slices
½ cup water	1 cup Kretschmer® wheat germ
1 teaspoon salt	
½ teaspoon oregano leaves, crushed	½ cup grated Parmesan cheese

Preheat oven to 375° F.

Sauté onion and garlic in oil until onion is tender. Add tomatoes, tomato paste, water, and seasonings. Simmer uncovered, 30 minutes.

Cook noodles as package directs for 10 minutes. Drain. Cover bottom of 9 by 13 by 2-inch baking pan with one-third of noodles. Dot with one-third of Ricotta cheese. Arrange one-third of Mozzarella slices over Ricotta. Sprinkle with one-third cup wheat germ over Mozzarella. Spread with one-third of sauce. Repeat layers two more times. Sprinkle with Parmesan cheese on top.

Bake for 25 to 30 minutes or until thoroughly heated. Let stand 10 minutes before cutting so filling will set slightly.

FRIED RICE

Makes 4 to 6 servings

3½–4 cups cooked long grain rice
3 tablespoons peanut or vegetable oil
1 egg
4 green onions with tops, sliced
1 clove garlic, minced
½ pound small shrimp, cleaned
½ cup sliced water chestnuts
¼ cup soy sauce
1 cup cooked green peas

Chill rice in refrigerator. In Farberware® electric wok, add 1 tablespoon of oil. Set heat control dial to 200° F. When light goes out, add egg and scramble; remove and set aside.

Turn heat control dial to 250° F. Add remaining oil, onion, and garlic. Stir-fry about 1 minute. Stir in shrimp and water chestnuts. Cook until shrimp curl and turn pink, about 4 minutes. Stir in cold rice and soy sauce until well mixed; stir in peas and egg. Stir constantly until hot.

Note: This dish can be prepared in advance and stored in 2-quart casserole in refrigerator. About 30 minutes before serving, heat uncovered in 350° F. oven. Cooked pork, beef, or chicken may be used instead of shrimp.

MEDITERRANEAN BROWN RICE SALAD

Makes 2 servings

½ medium tomato, seeded and chopped
1 sliced green onion
1–2 tablespoons chopped fresh parsley
1 cup cooked brown rice
⅓ cup Kretschmer® wheat germ
¼ cup plain low-fat yogurt
1 tablespoon lemon juice
Pepper to taste

Combine all ingredients; mix well. Cover and chill. Serve in green pepper or tomato cup, if desired.

HARVEST RICE

Makes about 12 cups

1 pound ground
    beef
1 pound ground
    pork
two 6-ounce
    packages
    long grain
    and wild rice
    mix, long
    cooking type

10-ounce package
    frozen peas
4⅔ cups water
⅓ cup chopped
    pecans
3 tablespoons
    butter or
    margarine

In Farberware® electric skillet with heat control set at 325° F., brown beef and pork until meat is no longer pink. Add rice mix, peas, and water. Cover and reduce heat to 220° F.

When water is absorbed and rice is tender, about 25 minutes, add pecans and butter. Turn heat control down until light goes out (simmer point). Simmer 5 minutes until done.

RICE PILAF

Makes 6 to 8 servings

2 tablespoons butter or margarine
1 cup chopped onion
1½ cups uncooked rice
¼ cup pignolia nuts or slivered almonds

5 chicken bouillon cubes
4 cups boiling water
1 tablespoon parsley flakes
¼ teaspoon garlic powder
¼ teaspoon black pepper

In Farberware® electric skillet, melt butter with heat control set at 300° F. Add onion, rice, and pignolia nuts. Sauté, stirring occasionally, until onion is soft and rice begins to brown.

Dissolve bouillon cubes in boiling water. Add to skillet. Stir in remaining ingredients. Cover and simmer at 220° F. until water is absorbed, about 30 minutes.

Fluff rice with fork and serve hot.

RICE ITALIAN STYLE

Makes 6 servings

1 cup uncooked white rice	2⅓ cups water
¼ cup chopped onion	½ cup Heinz tomato ketchup
1 teaspoon oregano leaves, crushed	1 teaspoon salt
	Dash pepper
2 tablespoons butter or margarine	Grated Parmesan cheese

In saucepan, sauté rice, onion, and oregano in butter stirring occasionally, until rice is golden brown.

Stir in water, ketchup, salt, and pepper; bring to boil. Cover; simmer 25 to 30 minutes or until rice is tender and liquid is absorbed.

Toss rice lightly with fork. Serve with a sprinkle of Parmesan cheese.

PASTA GARDENA

Makes 4 to 6 servings

8 ounces spaghetti or other pasta
½ cup vegetable oil
⅓ cup Heinz distilled white vinegar
2 cups cherry tomatoes, halved
½ cup chopped fresh parsley
¼ cup chopped fresh basil or 2 tablespoons dried basil
Dash salt
Dash pepper
½ cup grated Parmesan cheese

Cook pasta following package directions; drain well.

Meanwhile, combine oil and vinegar in jar; cover and shake vigorously.

In large skillet, combine cooked pasta, oil-vinegar mixture, and tomatoes. Heat over low heat, tossing gently. Add parsley, basil, salt, and pepper. Heat thoroughly.

Sprinkle each serving with Parmesan cheese.

Cakes, Pies, and Muffins

TART LEMON CHEESECAKE

Makes 8 servings

11¾-ounce package Royal® no bake cheesecake

⅓ cup margarine

5 tablespoons sugar

2 cups sour cream

1 cup milk

1 tablespoon lemon juice

2 teaspoons grated lemon peel

Lemon twists, for garnish

Mix crumb packet, 3 tablespoons sugar, and margarine; press on bottom and side of 9-inch pie plate. Prepare cheesecake filling according to package directions using 1 cup sour cream, milk, lemon juice, and lemon peel. Spread in prepared crust.

Blend remaining sour cream and sugar; spread over filling. Chill at least 2 hours.

Garnish with lemon twists if desired.

PUMPKIN CHEESECAKE

Makes 8 servings

11-ounce package
 Royal® no
 bake
 cheesecake
⅓ cup margarine,
 melted
3 tablespoons
 sugar
3-ounce package
 Royal® lemon
 gelatin
⅔ cup boiling
 water

1½ cups milk
1 cup solid pack
 canned
 pumpkin
1 teaspoon ground
 cinnamon
¼ teaspoon ground
 ginger
Whipped cream
 and chopped
 pecans, for
 garnish

Prepare graham cracker crust according to package directions in 9-inch pie plate using margarine and sugar; set aside.

In small bowl, dissolve gelatin in boiling water; cool to room temperature.

In medium bowl, prepare cheesecake filling according to package directions using a mixture of milk, cooled gelatin, pumpkin, cinnamon, and ginger. Chill until mixture mounds.

Spoon into pie plate. Chill until firm, about 3 hours.

To serve, garnish with whipped cream and chopped pecans if desired.

DOUBLE CHOCOLATE CHEESECAKE

Makes 8 servings

11¾-ounce package Royal® no bake cheesecake
½ cup margarine, melted
½ cup sugar
1 cup semisweet chocolate chips

1½ cups cold milk
4⅛-ounce package Royal® chocolate pudding and pie filling
1¾ cups water
Whipped cream, for garnish

Cheesecake: Mix crumb packet, 6 tablespoons margarine, and 2 tablespoons sugar; press on bottom and side of 9-inch pie plate.

In small saucepan, over low heat, melt ½ cup chocolate chips; set aside. Prepare cheesecake filling according to package directions using milk; blend in melted chocolate. Stir in remaining chocolate chips. Spread in prepared crust. Chill 1 hour.

Sauce: In small saucepan, over medium-high heat, heat pudding, remaining sugar, and water to a boil. Boil 1 minute; remove from heat. Stir in remaining margarine. Chill until serving time.

To serve, cut cheesecake into 8 wedges; top with sauce and whipped cream if desired.

STRAWBERRY RIBBON CHEESECAKE

Makes 12 servings

1 graham cracker crushed

8-ounce tub light pasteurized process cream cheese product

⅔ cup strawberry jam or preserves

3¼ cups (8 ounces) Cool Whip® Lite Whipped Topping, thawed

6 fresh strawberries, halved

Spray 8- or 9-inch springform pan or pie plate with no-stick cooking spray. Dust with graham cracker crumbs; set aside.

Beat cream cheese product and ⅓ cup jam. Stir in 2 cups whipped topping. Pour into prepared pan; smooth top. Freeze 3 to 4 hours or until firm.

To serve, remove from freezer; spread remaining ⅓ cup jam over top. Top with remaining whipped topping. Garnish with strawberries.

LEMON POPPYSEED CHEESECAKE

Makes 8 servings

1 cup Kretschmer®
　Original or
　honey crunch
　wheat germ
2 tablespoons
　sugar
2 tablespoons
　margarine,
　melted
1 tablespoon
　grated lemon
　peel
　16-ounce carton
　plain nonfat
　yogurt

8-ounce package
　Neufchâtel
　cheese (light
　cream cheese)
¾ cup sugar
2 egg whites
2 tablespoons poppy
　seeds
1 tablespoon grated
　lemon peel
1 tablespoon
　cornstarch

Preheat oven to 350° F.

Combine wheat germ, sugar, margarine, and lemon peel; press onto bottom of 9-inch springform pan. Bake about 15 minutes.

Increase over temperature to 400° F. Combine remaining ingredients; mix at medium speed with electric mixer until well blended. Pour over crust and bake 10 minutes.

Lower heat to 350° F and bake 40 minutes or until set; cool.

Chill before serving. Store in refrigerator.

MOIST AND MINTY BROWNIES

Makes 16

1¼ cups all-purpose
flour
½ teaspoon
baking soda
¼ teaspoon salt
¾ cup sugar
½ cup (1 stick)
butter
2 tablespoons
water

10-ounce package
(1½ cups)
Nestlé® Toll
House® mint
flavored semi-
sweet chocolate
morsels, divided
1 teaspoon vanilla
extract
2 eggs

Preheat oven to 350° F.

In small bowl, combine flour, baking soda, and salt; set aside.

In small saucepan, combine sugar, butter, and water. Bring *just to a boil*; remove from heat. Or, combine ingredients in bowl. Microwave on high 1½ minutes; stir. Microwave on high 1½ minutes longer; stir until smooth. Add 1 cup chocolate morsels and vanilla extract, stirring until morsels are melted and mixture is smooth. Transfer to large bowl.

Add eggs, one at a time, beating well with electric beater after each addition. Stir in flour mixture and remaining chocolate morsels. Spread in greased 9-inch square baking pan.

Bake 25 to 35 minutes, just until center is set. Cool completely. Cut into 2¼-inch squares.

MINI MORSEL CUPCAKES

Makes 24

Cupcakes:

2½ cups all-purpose flour
2 teaspoons baking powder
½ teaspoon salt
1 cup (2 sticks) butter, softened
1½ cups sugar
2 teaspoons vanilla extract
4 eggs
1 cup milk
12-ounce package (2 cups) Nestlé® Toll House® semi-sweet chocolate mini morsels, divided

Frosting:

1 cup Nestlé® Toll House® semi-sweet chocolate mini morsels (reserved from cupcakes)
2½ cups sifted confectioner's sugar
½ cup (1 stick) butter, softened
¼ cup milk
1 teaspoon vanilla extract

Preheat oven to 375° F.

Cupcakes:

In small bowl, combine flour, baking powder, and salt; set aside.

In large bowl, with electric beater beat butter, sugar, and vanilla extract until creamy. Add eggs, one at a time, beating well after each addition. Gradually blend in flour mixture alternately with milk (batter may appear curdled). Stir in 1 cup chocolate mini morsels. Spoon batter into 24 paper-lined muffin cups, filling each ¾ full.

Bake 18 to 22 minutes or until tops spring back when lightly pressed. Cool completely.

Frosting:

Melt remaining 1 cup chocolate mini morsels; let cool. In small bowl, beat confectioner's sugar, butter, milk, vanilla extract, and melted chocolate until creamy. Spread over cooled cupcakes.

If desired, frost cupcakes with your favorite frosting. Sprinkle remaining 1 cup chocolate mini morsels over cupcakes to decorate.

Cake Mix Shortcut: Add ½ cup all-purpose flour to cake mix; prepare according to package directions. Stir in 1 cup chocolate mini morsels. Bake as directed.

STRAWBERRY SEVEN LAYER CAKE

Makes 6 to 8 servings

2 pound frozen pound cake, partially thawed

2 cups Welch's squeezable strawberry spread

With long serrated knife, slice lengthwise pound cake into 6 thin layers. Spread each layer with about ⅓ cup strawberry spread. Chill about 1 hour.

Serve with sweetened whipped cream, if desired.

MICROWAVE PEANUT BUTTER AND JAM CAKE

Makes 12 servings

2 eggs, slightly
   beaten
½ cup peanut
   butter
3½ cups (8
   ounces)
   Cool Whip®
   whipped
   topping,
   thawed

1½ cups graham
   cracker
   crumbs
¼ cup sugar
⅓ cup grape jam
⅓ cup chopped
   peanuts

Mix eggs and peanut butter in large bowl. Stir in whipped topping, crumbs and sugar. Spread in greased 8-inch square or 1½ quart round micro-waveable dish.

Cook on medium (50 percent) for 5 minutes. Rotate dish half turn; cook on high 4½ to 5½ minutes more or until cake starts to pull away from edges and is slightly moist.

Immediately place serving plate over dish; invert. Spread cake with jam; sprinkle with peanuts.

COOKIES AND CREAM PIE

Makes 6 to 8 servings

1½ cups cold light cream
4-serving-size package vanilla flavor instant pudding and pie filling

3½ cups (8 ounces) Cool Whip® whipped topping, thawed
1 cup chopped chocolate sandwich cookies
1 packaged 9 inch chocolate crumb crust

Pour light cream into large mixing bowl. Add pie filling mix. Beat with wire whisk until well blended, approximately 1 minute. Let stand 5 minutes.

Fold in whipped topping and cookie crumbs. Spoon into purchased crust.

Freeze until firm, about 6 hours or overnight. Remove from freezer. Let stand about 10 minutes to soften before serving. Store any leftover pie in freezer.

CHOCO-MINT PIE

Makes 6 to 8 servings

1½ cups cold half and half or milk

4-serving-size package chocolate flavor instant pudding and pie filling

3½ cups (8 ounces) Cool Whip® whipped topping, thawed

1 cup chopped chocolate covered mint sandwich cookies (7 to 8 cookies)

1 packaged 9 inch chocolate cookie crumb crust

Pour half and half into large mixing bowl. Add pie filling mix. Beat with wire whisk until well blended, approximately 1 minute. Let stand 5 minutes.

Fold in whipped topping and chopped cookies. Spoon into purchased crust.

Freeze until firm, about 6 hours or overnight. Remove from freezer. Let stand about 10 minutes to soften before serving. Store any leftover pie in freezer.

PEACH CHEESE PIE

Makes 6 to 8 servings

8-ounce package
cream cheese,
softened
2 tablespoons
sugar
2 tablespoons milk
3 cups Cool Whip®
whipped topping,
thawed
9-inch graham
cracker crumb
crust or pie
shell, baked
and cooled

2 medium
peaches,
peeled, pitted,
and diced
4- serving-size
package
vanilla or
lemon flavor
instant
pudding and
pie filling
1¼ cups cold milk
¼ teaspoon almond
extract

Beat cream cheese until smooth; blend in sugar and 2 tablespoons milk. Fold in 2 cups of the whipped topping and spread in crust. Top with peach slices, pressing down lightly. Chill.

Prepare pie filling mix with 1¼ cups milk as directed on package. Add almond extract and let stand 5 minutes. Fold in remaining whipped topping and spoon over cheese mixture.

Chill 3 hours (or place in freezer for 30 minutes; then chill 2 hours). Garnish with additional whipped topping and peach slices, if desired.

BOSTON CREAM PIE

Makes 6 to 8 servings

3⅜-ounce package Royal® instant vanilla pudding and pie filling

1½ cups cold milk

9-inch yellow cake layer, baked and cooled, split horizontally

2 ounces unsweetened chocolate (2 squares)

2 tablespoons margarine

1 cup confectioner's sugar

½ teaspoon vanilla extract

4–5 tablespoons hot water

Prepare pudding mix according to package directions using milk; spread between split cake layer.

In small saucepan, over low heat, blend chocolate and margarine, stirring until chocolate melts; remove from heat. Blend in sugar and vanilla. Gradually stir in enough hot water until glaze consistency is reached. Drizzle glaze over top of cake.

TWO-TONE FRUIT PIE

Makes 8 servings

1½ cups graham cracker crumbs
¼ cup sugar
⅓ cup margarine, melted
6-ounce package Royal® strawberry gelatin (or two 3-ounce packages)

1½ cups boiling water
1 cup sour cream
¾ cup cold water
Prepared whipped topping, strawberry slices, and blueberries, for garnish

In bowl, combine crumbs, sugar, and margarine; press on bottom and side of 9-inch pie plate. Set aside.

Dissolve gelatin in boiling water. Blend ¾ cup dissolved gelatin with sour cream; chill 20 minutes. Spoon into prepared crust. Meanwhile, stir cold water into remaining dissolved gelatin; chill until thickened, about 20 minutes. Carefully spoon over sour cream layer. Chill until firm, about 4 hours.

To serve, garnish with whipped topping and fruit.

TOLL HOUSE™ PIE

Makes 6 to 8 servings

2 eggs
½ cup all-purpose
    flour
½ cup sugar
½ cup firmly
    packed light
    brown sugar
¾ cup (1½ sticks)
    butter,
    softened

one 6-ounce
    package (1
    cup) Nestlé®
    Toll House®
    semi-sweet
    chocolate
    morsels
1 cup chopped
    walnuts
9-inch unbaked
    pie shell*
Whipped cream
    or ice cream,
    optional

Preheat oven to 325° F.

In large bowl, with electric beater beat eggs at high speed until foamy, about 3 minutes. Beat in flour, sugar, and brown sugar until well blended. Beat in softened butter. Stir in chocolate morsels and walnuts. Pour into pie shell.

Bake 55 to 60 minutes or until knife inserted halfway between edge and center comes out clean, and top is golden brown. Cool on wire rack.

Serve with whipped cream or ice cream, if desired.

---

*If using frozen pie shell, use deep-dish style; thaw completely. Place on cookie sheet; increase baking time by 10 minutes.

CHOCOLATE WALNUT TART

Makes 8 servings

1 refrigerated pie crust

¼ cup firmly packed brown sugar

2 eggs

½ cup Grandma's® molasses (Gold Label)

1 cup chopped walnuts

2 tablespoons margarine or butter, melted

¼ cup semisweet chocolate chips, melted

Preheat oven to 450° F.

Prepare pie crust according to package directions for unfilled one-crust pie using 9-inch tart pan with removable bottom. Bake for 9 to 11 minutes or until light brown. Cool.

Reduce oven temperature to 350° F. In medium bowl, beat brown sugar and eggs until fluffy. Add molasses, walnuts, and margarine; mix well. Pour into cooled, baked crust. Bake for 35 to 45 minutes or until filling is set. Cool. Drizzle melted chocolate over top. Store in refrigerator.

FRESH FRUIT TART

Makes 6 servings

2½ cups toasted
    coconut
⅓ cup melted
    butter
15 ounces low-fat
    ricotta
    cheese
 2 teaspoons
    freshly grated
    lemon rind

1 teaspoon vanilla
    extract
⅓ cup Welch's
    purple grape
    juice
Assortment of
    summer fruit

Combine coconut and butter. Press coconut into a 9-inch tart or pie pan to form a crust. Chill.

In a mixing bowl combine ricotta, lemon rind, vanilla, and grape juice; mix until well blended. Pour cheese filling into chilled crust. Chill for several hours or overnight. For quick chilling, place tart in the freezer for 2 hours.

Just before serving, attractively arrange fresh fruit over the tart.

MIX-A-MUFFIN

Makes 12 muffins

1½ cups all-purpose flour
½ cups regular, Instant or Quick Cream of Wheat®
4 teaspoons baking powder

¾ cup milk
½ cup firmly packed light brown sugar
⅓ cup margarine, melted
1 egg
1 teaspoon vanilla extract

Preheat oven to 400° F.

In large bowl, mix flour, cereal, and baking powder. In medium bowl, whisk together milk, brown sugar, margarine, egg, and vanilla. Make a well in center of flour mixture; stir in milk mixture just until blended (batter will be lumpy). Let stand 5 minutes. Spoon batter into 12 greased 2½-inch muffin pan cups.

Bake for 15 to 20 minutes until done. Cool in pan on wire rack for 5 minutes. Remove from pan, cool on wire rack. Serve warm.

FRUIT MUFFINS

Makes 12 muffins

1 cup Kretschmer®
original
wheat germ
or honey
crunch wheat
germ
1 cup all-purpose
flour
⅓ cup sugar
1 tablespoon
baking powder

1 cup skim milk
1 cup blueberries,
mashed
banana, or
chopped apple
¼ cup vegetable oil
2 egg whites,
slightly beaten
1 teaspoon ground
cinnamon

Preheat oven to 400° F. Line 12 medium muffin cups with paper baking cups or lightly grease bottoms only with no-stick cooking spray. Combine first 4 ingredients. Add combined remaining ingredients, mixing just until dry ingredients are moistened. Fill prepared muffin cups almost full.

Bake 20 to 25 minutes or until golden brown. Store tightly wrapped in freezer.

To reheat, microwave on high about 30 seconds per muffin.

APPLE WHOLE WHEAT MUFFINS

Makes 12 muffins

1¼ cups all-purpose flour
¾ cup whole wheat flour
⅓ cup sugar
1 tablespoon baking powder
1 teaspoon ground cinnamon
½ teaspoon ground ginger

⅔ cup undiluted Carnation® evaporated lowfat milk
⅓ cup apple juice
¼ cup vegetable oil
1 egg
1¼ cups (1 large) peeled, finely diced apple
1 tablespoon sugar
½ teaspoon ground cinnamon

Preheat oven to 400° F.

In medium bowl, combine flours, ⅓ cup sugar, baking powder, 1 teaspoon cinnamon, and ginger. In small bowl, combine milk, apple juice, oil, and egg; beat to blend in egg. Add liquid ingredients to dry ingredients; stir just until moistened. Fold in apples.

Spoon batter into 12 paper-lined muffin cups. Combine 1 tablespoon granulated sugar and ½ teaspoon ground cinnamon. Sprinkle mixture over muffins. Bake for 15 minutes or until toothpick inserted in center comes out clean. Remove from muffin tin to cool.

JUMBO JAM MUFFINS

Makes 9 muffins

12-ounce package
corn muffin
mix
⅔ cup milk
1 egg
⅓ cup miniature
chocolate chips

22-ounce bottle
Welch's grape
jelly or
raspberry apple
spread

Preheat oven to 400° F.

Prepare muffin mix according to package directions using milk and egg; stir in chocolate chips. Spoon half the batter into nine cupcake-paper-lined muffin tins. Squeeze in about 2 teaspoons grape jelly or raspberry apple spread. Spoon remaining batter over filling. Bake 20 to 22 minutes.

If desired, squeeze additional jelly on top of muffins. Cool slightly before serving.

PEANUT BUTTER AND JAM MUFFINS

Makes 12 muffins

2 cups flour
⅓ cup sugar
1 tablespoon
baking
powder
½ teaspoon salt
½ cup peanut butter

1 cup milk
1 egg
¼ cup vegetable oil
¼ cup Welch's
grape jam

Preheat oven to 400° F.

In bowl combine flour, sugar, baking powder, and salt. Add peanut butter; mix until crumbly. Add milk, egg, and oil; mix just until blended. Spoon half of the batter into 12 paper-lined muffin tin cups, dividing equally. Spoon 1 teaspoon jam into center of each muffin. Cover with remaining batter.

Bake for 18 to 20 minutes, until lightly browned and springy to the touch.

Serve warm or at room temperature.

GINGERBREAD STREUSEL RAISIN MUFFINS

Makes 12 muffins

1 cup raisins	½ teaspoon salt
½ cup boiling water	1 teaspoon cinnamon
⅓ cup margarine or butter, softened	1 teaspoon ginger
¾ cup Grandma's® molasses (Gold Label)	⅓ cup all-purpose flour
1 egg	¼ cup firmly packed brown sugar
2 cups all-purpose flour	3 tablespoons margarine or butter
1½ teaspoons baking soda	1 teaspoon cinnamon
	¼ cup chopped nuts

Preheat oven to 375° F.

Grease bottoms only of 12 muffin cups or line with paper baking cups. In small bowl, cover raisins with boiling water; let stand 5 minutes. In large bowl, beat ⅓ cup margarine and molasses until light. Add egg; beat well. Stir in 2 cups flour, baking soda, salt, cinnamon, and ginger. Blend just until dry ingredients are moistened. Gently stir in raisins and water. Fill prepared muffin cups three fourths full.

In small bowl, combine ⅓ cup flour, brown sugar, margarine, cinnamon, and nuts. Sprinkle over batter.

Bake for 20 to 25 minutes or until toothpick inserted in center comes out clean.

Cool 5 minutes; remove from pan. Serve warm.

CONCORD GRAPE-NUT BREAD

Makes 1 loaf

2 cups flour	½ cup chopped walnuts
1 teaspoon baking powder	1 cup milk
1 teaspoon baking soda	1 egg
½ teaspoon salt	½ cup sugar
6 tablespoons chopped candied fruits (citron, cherries, pineapple)	1 tablespoon melted butter or margarine
	½ cup Welch's grape jam

Preheat oven to 350° F. Line a greased 9 by 5-inch loaf pan with greased brown paper.

Combine flour, baking powder, baking soda, salt, candied fruits, and nuts in a mixing bowl. Combine milk, egg, sugar, and butter in another bowl, stirring briefly. Mix and combine liquids with dry ingredients. Stir briefly.

Pour one half batter into greased loaf pan. Pour jam over batter in a strip down the middle. Pour remaining batter over jam.

Bake for about 55 minutes or until bread tests done. Cool 15 minutes on wire rack before removing from pan. Cut when completely cool.

JAM POCKETS

10-ounce can
    buttermilk
    biscuit dough
1 jar Welch's
    strawberry or
    raspberry
    apple spread

Vegetable oil
Sugar

Using hands, flatten each biscuit. Place about 1 teaspoon spread on each. Fold over to form a pocket; press to seal.

In medium skillet with about 1-inch hot oil, fry each pocket about 3 minutes, turning frequently. Drain on paper towel. Roll in sugar.

Cookies and Fudge

JAM-STRIPED COCOA BARS

Makes about 36

1 cup butter or
    margarine
¾ cup
    unsweetened
    cocoa
1¾ cups sugar
1½ teaspoons
    vanilla
    extract
3 eggs
1¼ cups all-purpose
    flour

½ teaspoon baking
    powder
¼ teaspoon salt
    Peanut Butter
    Frosting (recipe
    follows)
¼ cup Welch's
    grape jelly

Preheat oven to 350° F.

Grease 9 by 13 by 2-inch baking pan.

In medium saucepan over low heat melt butter; add cocoa, stirring until smooth. Remove from heat; cool slightly.

Add sugar, vanilla, and eggs; beat with spoon until well blended. Add flour, baking powder, and salt; mix well. Spread batter into prepared pan.

Bake 25 to 30 minutes or until top is dry and wooden pick inserted in center comes out clean. Cool. Spread Peanut Butter Frosting over top. With end of spoon handle score diagonal ridges in frosting about 1½ inches apart. Heat jelly until melted; spoon into ridges. Allow to set until jelly is set. Cut into bars.

Peanut Butter Frosting

¼ cup butter or margarine

3 tablespoons milk

1 cup peanut butter chips

½ teaspoon vanilla extract

¾ cup powdered sugar

In small saucepan combine butter, milk, and peanut butter chips. Cook over low heat, stirring constantly, until mixture is smooth. Stir in vanilla. In small bowl combine hot mixture with powdered sugar; beat until thickened. Use immediately.

NATURALLY SWEET SNACK BARS

Makes 16

2 tablespoons butter or margarine
⅓ cup white grape juice
2 cups rolled oats, toasted
¾ cup fruit bits
½ cup chopped toasted pecans
1 teaspoon ground cinnamon
1 egg, beaten
½ cup mashed banana (1 small, ripe banana)
⅓ cup Welch's strawberry spread

Preheat oven to 350° F. Grease 9-inch square baking pan.

In small saucepan over low heat melt butter in grape juice. In large bowl stir together oats, fruit bits, pecans, and cinnamon. Pour juice mixture over oat mixture. Add egg and banana; stir until well blended. Press mixture into prepared pan.

Bake 25 to 30 minutes or until edges are golden brown. Immediately smooth strawberry spread over top. Cool slightly; cut into squares.

Note: To toast oats and pecans, preheat oven to 350° F. Spread oats in large baking pan; toast 15 to 20 minutes, stirring occasionally, until lightly browned. Cool. Heat oven to 375° F. Spread ½ cup pecan halves or pieces in single layer in shallow baking pan; toast 5 to 7 minutes, stirring occasionally, until lightly browned. (Do not overtoast.) Cool thoroughly before chopping.

CHOCOLATE PEANUT CRUNCH

Makes 4 servings

4 teaspoons dry roasted peanuts, chopped

4⅛-ounce package Royal® instant chocolate pudding and pie filling (or a 3⅜-ounce package pistachio or vanilla)

1¾ cups heavy cream

3 chocolate sandwich cookies, finely chopped (about ¼ cup)

Whipped cream, grated chocolate, and maraschino cherries, for garnish

Spoon 1 teaspoon chopped peanuts in bottom of each of four lightly oiled 4-ounce molds; set aside.

In bowl, with electric mixer at low speed, beat pudding mix and heavy cream for 1 minute. Spoon half the pudding over peanuts, firmly pressing into each mold; sprinkle evenly with cookie crumbs. Spread remaining pudding over cookie crumbs. Freeze until firm, about 3 hours.

Using tip of knife, loosen the pudding from the edges of the mold; dip in warm water for 30 seconds. Unmold onto serving plate; let stand 10 minutes at room temperature before serving. Garnish with whipped cream, grated chocolate, and maraschino cherries.

TOLL HOUSE™ BLONDIES

Makes about 35

2¼ cups all-purpose
    flour
2½ teaspoons
    baking
    powder
½ teaspoon salt
¾ cup (1½ sticks)
    butter, softened
1¾ cups firmly
    packed
    brown sugar

3 eggs
1 teaspoon vanilla
    extract
12-ounce package
    (2 cups) Nestlé®
    Toll House®
    semi-sweet
    chocolate
    morsels

Preheat oven to 350° F.

In small bowl, combine flour, baking powder, and salt; set aside.

In large bowl, with electric beater, beat butter and sugar until creamy. Beat in eggs and vanilla extract. Gradually blend in flour mixture. Stir in chocolate morsels. Spread in greased 10½ by 15½ by 1-inch baking pan.

Bake 20 to 25 minutes or until top is golden brown. Cool. Cut into 2-inch squares.

Variation: Preheat oven to 350° F. Spread batter in greased 9 by 13 by 2-inch baking pan. Bake 30 to 35 minutes or until top is golden brown. Cool. Cut into 2-inch squares. Makes about 24 squares.

CHOCOLATE MACAROON SQUARES

Makes 24

18¼-ounce package chocolate cake mix
⅓ cup butter or margarine, softened
1 egg, lightly beaten
1¼ cups (14-ounce can) Carnation® sweetened condensed milk

1 teaspoon vanilla extract
1 egg
1⅓ cups flaked sweetened coconut, divided
1 cup chopped pecans
1 cup (6-ounce package) Nestlé® Toll House® semisweet chocolate morsels

Preheat oven to 350° F.

In large bowl, combine cake mix, butter, and 1 egg; mix with fork until crumbly. Press firmly into even layer in bottom of 9 by 13 by 2-inch baking pan; set aside.

In medium bowl, combine condensed milk, vanilla, and 1 egg; beat until well blended. Stir in 1 cup coconut, pecans, and chocolate morsels. Spread mixture evenly over dough; sprinkle with remaining coconut.

Bake for about 30 minutes or until center is almost set. (Center will be set when cool.) Cool on wire rack. Cut into 2-inch squares.

PEANUT BUTTER COOKIES

Makes 48

⅔ cups firmly packed light brown sugar

½ cup chunky or creamy peanut butter

⅓ cup margarine, softened

1 egg

½ cup regular, Instant, or Quick Cream of Wheat® cereal

1 teaspoon vanilla extract

1¼ cups all-purpose flour

½ teaspoon baking soda

Preheat oven to 350° F.

In medium bowl, with electric mixer at medium speed, beat brown sugar, peanut butter, margarine, and egg until fluffy; blend in cereal and vanilla. Stir in flour and baking soda to make a stiff dough.

Roll dough into 1-inch balls; place 2 inches apart on greased baking sheets. Flatten balls with bottom of a floured glass; press with fork tines to make crisscross pattern.

Bake for 8 to 9 minutes or until lightly browned. Remove from sheets; cool on wire racks.

DOUBLE CHOCOLATE DREAM COOKIES

Makes about 42

2¼ cups all-
   purpose
   flour
½ cup Nestlé®
   cocoa
1 teaspoon
   baking soda
½ teaspoon salt
1 cup (2 sticks)
   butter or
   margarine,
   softened

1 cup firmly packed
   brown sugar
¾ cup sugar
1 teaspoon vanilla
   extract
2 eggs
12-ounce package
   (2 cups)
   Nestlé® Toll
   House® semi-
   sweet chocolate
   morsels

Preheat oven to 375° F.

In small bowl, combine flour, cocoa, baking soda, and salt; set aside.

In large bowl, with electric beater beat butter, brown sugar, sugar, and vanilla extract until creamy. Beat in eggs until light and fluffy, about 2 minutes. Gradually blend in flour mixture. Stir in chocolate morsels.

Drop by rounded measuring tablespoonfuls onto ungreased cookie sheets.

Bake 8 to 10 minutes or until cookies are puffed. Let stand on cookie sheets 2 minutes. Remove from cookie sheets; cool.

OATMEAL SCOTCHIES

Makes about 48

1¼ cups all-purpose
  flour
1 teaspoon
  baking soda
½ teaspoon salt
½ teaspoon
  cinnamon
1 cup (2 sticks)
  butter,
  softened
¾ cup sugar
¾ cup firmly
  packed
  brown sugar

2 eggs
1 teaspoon vanilla
  extract or grated
  peel of 1 orange
3 cups quick or old-
  fashioned oats,
  uncooked
12-ounce package
  (2 cups) Nestlé®
  Toll House®
  butterscotch
  flavored morsels

Preheat oven to 375° F.

In small bowl, combine flour, baking soda, salt, and cinnamon; set aside.

In large bowl, with electric beater, beat butter, sugar, brown sugar, eggs, and vanilla extract or orange peel until creamy. Gradually beat in flour mixture. Stir in oats and butterscotch morsels.

Drop by measuring tablespoonfuls onto ungreased cookie sheets.

Bake 7 to 8 minutes for chewier cookies; 9 to 10 minutes for crisper cookies. Let stand on cookie sheets 2 minutes. Remove from cookie sheets; cool.

Oatmeal Scotchie Pan Cookies

Preheat oven to 375° F. Spread dough in greased 10½ by 15½ by 1-inch baking pan. Bake 18 to 22 minutes until very lightly browned. Cool completely. Cut into 2-inch squares. Makes about 35 squares.

FIVE MINUTE FUDGE

Makes 2 pounds

2 tablespoons butter or margarine
⅔ cup undiluted Carnation® evaporated milk
1⅔ cups sugar
½ teaspoon salt
2 cups (4 ounces) miniature marshmallows

1½ cups (1½ 6-ounce packages) Nestlé® Toll House semisweet chocolate morsels
1 teaspoon vanilla
½ cup chopped pecans or walnuts

In medium saucepan, combine butter, evaporated milk, sugar, and salt. Bring to a boil over medium heat, stirring constantly. Boil 4 to 5 minutes, stirring constantly. Remove from heat. Stir in marshmallows, chocolate chips, vanilla, and nuts. Stir vigorously for 1 minute or until marshmallows melt and blend. Pour into buttered 8-inch-square pan. Cool. Cut into squares.

Fancy Fudge

Omit chopped nuts. Substitute ¼ cup toasted chopped almonds and ½ cup finely chopped candied mixed fruit.

Five-Minute Fudge Rolls

Make fudge as directed. Spread about 1 cup chopped nuts on waxed paper. Pour fudge mixture over nuts. As fudge cools, form into roll. Slice.

Peppermint Fudge

Sprinkle ¼ cup coarsely broken peppermint candy over top of fudge in pan.

Upside Down Coconut Fudge

Spread 1 cup flaked, toasted coconut on bottom of buttered 8-inch-square pan. Top with fudge.

Peanut Fudge

Substitute ½ cup chopped peanuts for nuts.

CREAMY CRUNCHY BARS

Makes 20

½-pound bag multicolored milk chocolate candies, chopped
½-pound bag multicolored milk chocolate peanut candies, chopped
⅓ cup oil
6 cups cocoa flavored dry cereal

1 cup cold milk
⅓ cup peanut butter
4-serving-size package vanilla or chocolate flavor instant pudding and pie filling
3½ cups (8 ounces) Cool Whip® whipped topping, thawed

In microwave oven heat candy and oil on high 1 minute; stir until candy is melted. Stir in cereal; toss to coat well. Press half the mixture into bottom of 9 by 13 by 2-inch greased foil-lined pan.

Mix milk and peanut butter in large bowl until smooth. Stir in pudding mix until well blended; mix in whipped topping. Spread over cereal mixture in pan. Top with remaining cereal mixture.

Freeze until firm, about 3 to 4 hours. Cut into bars.

CHOCOLATE PEANUT BUTTER TRUFFLES

Makes about 30

8-ounces
   semisweet
   chocolate
½ cup peanut
   butter
3 cups (8 ounces)
   Cool Whip®
   extra creamy
   whipped topping,
   thawed

Crushed vanilla
   wafers, chopped
   nuts, or toasted
   coconut, for
   garnish

In microwave oven heat chocolate in micro-waveable bowl on high 3 minutes, stirring halfway through heating time. Remove from microwave oven; stir until completely melted.

Mix in peanut butter until smooth; cool to room temperature. Gently stir in whipped topping; refrigerate 1 hour.

Roll into 1-inch balls; coat with vanilla wafers, nuts, or coconut.

CHOCOLATE PEANUT BUDDY BARS

Makes 48

1 cup peanut butter
6 tablespoons (¾ stick) butter or margarine, softened
1¼ cups sugar
3 eggs
1 teaspoon vanilla extract
1 cup all-purpose flour
¼ teaspoon salt
11½-ounce package (2 cups) Nestlé® Toll House® milk chocolate morsels, divided

Preheat oven to 350° F.

In large bowl, with electric beater beat peanut butter and butter until smooth, about 1 minute. Beat in sugar, eggs, and vanilla extract until creamy. Blend in flour and salt. Stir in 1 cup milk chocolate morsels. Spread in ungreased 9 by 13 by 2-inch baking pan.

Bake 25 to 30 minutes until edges begin to brown. Immediately sprinkle remaining milk chocolate morsels over cookie layer. Let stand 5 minutes or until morsels become shiny and soft. Spread morsels evenly over top. Cool completely. Cut into 1½ inch bars.

WHITE FUDGE

Makes about 2 pounds

7-ounce jar marshmallow cream
1½ cups sugar
⅔ cup evaporated milk
¼ cup (½ stick) butter
¼ teaspoon salt

two 6-ounce packages (6 foil-wrapped bars) Nestlé® Premier White™ baking bars, broken up
½ cup chopped nuts
1 teaspoon vanilla extract

In 2-quart heavy saucepan, combine marshmallow cream, sugar, evaporated milk, butter, and salt. Bring to full rolling boil over moderate heat, stirring constantly. Boil 5 minutes, stirring constantly. Remove from heat.

Stir in white baking bars until melted and smooth. Stir in nuts and vanilla extract.

Pour into greased 8-inch-square pan. Refrigerate until firm about 2 hours.

Cut into squares.

Delicious Desserts

PEACH BLUEBERRY TRIFLE

Makes 12 servings

1¼ cups (14-ounce can) Carnation® sweetened condensed milk

1½ cups cold water

3½-ounce package vanilla *instant* pudding and pie filling mix

1 cup heavy cream, whipped

1 pound cake (approximately 10 to 12 ounces) cut into 1-inch strips or cubes

2 cups (approximately 1 pound) fresh, ripe, peaches, peeled and cut into 1-inch cubes

2 cups fresh blueberries

Fresh fruit garnish

In large bowl, with electric mixer beat sweetened condensed milk and water until blended. Add pudding mix; beat on medium speed 2 to 3 minutes, or until thickened. Chill 10 minutes.

Fold whipped cream into pudding. To assemble, in 3 or 4-quart trifle bowl or large glass serving bowl, spoon 2 cups pudding mixture. Layer half cake cubes, all the peaches, half of the remaining pudding. Repeat procedure using all the blueberries. Cover and chill at least 1 hour before serving.

Note: 16-ounce can sliced peaches or 16-ounce package frozen sliced peaches, drained and cut into 1-inch cubes or 10-ounce package frozen, thawed blueberries may be substituted.

MIX-UP STICKS

Makes about 30

18 large marshmallows
2 tablespoons milk
2 squares unsweetened chocolate, chopped
3½ cups (8 ounces) Cool Whip® whipped topping, thawed

Bananas, cut in 2-inch chunks or large marshmallows
Chopped chocolate sandwich cookies
Chopped nuts
Toasted flake coconut

In microwave oven heat marshmallows with milk in microwaveable bowl on high 1½ minutes until melted; beat with wire whisk until smooth.

Stir in chocolate until melted. Add whipped topping; mix well.

Place banana chunk or marshmallow on ends of wooden sticks. Coat with chocolate mixture; then roll in cookies, nuts, or coconut.

Refrigerate 1 hour before serving.

CHOCOLATE MOLASSES CUPS

Makes 36

3 refrigerated pie crusts
½ cup Grandma's® molasses (Gold Label)
2 eggs
¼ cup sugar

6-ounce package (1 cup) Nestlé® Toll House semisweet chocolate chips
½ cup chopped walnuts
Confectioner's sugar

Allow crusts to sit at room temperature for 15 to 20 minutes. Preheat oven to 350° F.

Unfold each pie crust; peel off top plastic sheets. Press out fold lines. Invert and remove remaining plastic sheets. Cut twelve 2½-inch circles from each pie crust. Press into bottom and sides of mini-muffin or muffin gem pan.

In medium bowl, combine molasses, eggs, and sugar; beat until smooth. Stir in chocolate chips and walnuts. Spoon into pastry lined cups, filling each ⅔ full.

Bake for 20 to 25 minutes or until filling is set. Cool completely. Remove from pans. Sprinkle with powdered sugar.

CREAMY BERRY BURRITOS

Makes 10

1 cup cold milk
  4-serving-size
    package
    vanilla flavor
    instant pudding
    and pie
    filling
3½ cups (8 ounce)
    Cool Whip®
    whipped
    topping,
    thawed

1 pint strawberries,
    chopped
½ cup sugar
1 tablespoon
    cinnamon
10 flour tortillas
    (about 7 inches
    in diameter)
½ cup (1 stick)
    margarine or
    butter, melted

Preheat oven to 350° F.

Pour milk into bowl. Add pudding mix. Whisk until well blended. Let stand 5 minutes; fold in 2 cups whipped topping. Stir in strawberries, reserving some for garnish.

Combine sugar and cinnamon. Brush both sides of tortillas with margarine; sprinkle one side with sugar mixture.

Bake on ungreased cookie sheet for 5 to 7 minutes or until bubbly; let stand 5 minutes.

Spoon pudding mixture into center of tortilla. Roll up. Top with reserved strawberries and remaining whipped topping.

FRUITED BREAD PUDDING

Makes 4 servings

1¼ cups skim milk
⅓ cup firmly packed brown sugar
3 egg whites, slightly beaten
1 teaspoon vanilla
1½ cups toasted whole wheat bread cubes (2 to 3 slices coarse textured bread)

½ cup Kretschmer® original or honey crunch wheat germ
½ cup mixed dried fruit bits
Low-fat vanilla yogurt or warm low-fat milk

Preheat oven to 350° F. Lightly spray 1½-quart casserole with no-stick cooking spray. Combine first 4 ingredients in casserole; gently stir in remaining ingredients except yogurt.

Bake on center oven rack 40 to 45 minutes or until knife inserted in center comes out clean and top is golden brown. Spoon into bowls. If desired, serve with yogurt or warm milk.

NO-MELT ICE CREAM

Makes about 5 cups

1 cup Welch's red
   grape juice
6-ounce package
   lemon flavor
   gelatin

1 quart strawberry
   ice cream,
   softened
Ice cream cones

In saucepan, bring juice to boil; stir in gelatin to dissolve. In bowl beat ice cream smooth. Gradually stir in gelatin mixture. Chill thoroughly to set. Scoop into ice cream cones or dessert dishes.

CHOCOLATE CHIP ICE CREAM

Makes about 2 quarts

4 cups half and half milk

1¼ cups (14-ounce can) Carnation® sweetened condensed milk

2½ teaspoons vanilla extract

1 cup (6 ounces) Nestlé® Toll House® semisweet chocolate minimorsels

In large bowl, combine half and half, condensed milk, and vanilla; mix well. Pour into ice cream maker. Freeze according to manufacturer's instructions adding chocolate morsels halfway through freezing period.

Variations: For strawberry, peach, or berry ice cream, in large bowl, combine 2 to 3 cups fruit pulp, ½ cup sugar, 3 cups half and half, and 1¼ cups condensed milk. Pour into ice cream maker. Freeze according to manufacturer's instructions. (If using sweetened frozen fruit or berries, omit sugar.)

HARVEST COMPOTE

Makes 4 to 6 servings

8-ounce package
    mixed dried
    fruits
¼ cup golden
    raisins
2 cups Welch's
    white grape
    juice

½ cup sugar
2 strips *each* lemon
    peel and orange
    peel
2 tablespoons lemon
    juice

Put mixed dried fruits and raisins in saucepan with grape juice, sugar, peels, and lemon juice. Bring to boil; reduce heat and simmer 15 minutes. Cool.

Store in covered container in refrigerator. Serve as an accompaniment to meats or over ice cream, puddings, or pound cake.

CARAMEL BAKED APPLES

Makes 4

1 tablespoon flour	¾ cup orange juice
1 regular (10 by 16-inch) Reynolds oven cooking bag	2 tablespoons honey
	4 large Rome apples
¼ teaspoon ground cinnamon	12 squares vanilla caramel candies

Preheat oven to 350° F.

Shake flour and cinnamon in cooking bag; place in 9 by 13 by 2-inch baking pan. Add orange juice to bag. Squeeze bag to blend ingredients. Add honey, continue to squeeze bag until well blended. Core apples, leaving a small plug in blossom end. Fill each apple with 3 caramels. Place apples in bag. Close bag with nylon tie; cut six ½-inch slits in top.

Bake 30 to 40 minutes or until apples are tender. Stir sauce; serve over apples.

Microwave Directions: Follow recipe as directed, except reduce orange juice to ¼ cup and pierce apples with a fork. Place bag in 8 by 8 by 2-inch microwave-safe baking dish. Close bag with nylon tie; cut six ½-inch slits in top. Rotating dish once after 4 minutes, microwave on high 7 to 9 minutes or until apples are tender. Let stand in bag 2 minutes.

PEACH MELBA MOLD

Makes 8 servings

⅔ cup Quick
 Cream of
 Wheat®
 cereal
3¼ cups milk
 16-ounce can
 sliced
 peaches,
 drained and
 chopped

½ cup sliced
 almonds,
 toasted and
 chopped
¼ cup honey
¼ teaspoon almond
 extract
½ cup raspberry jam

Prepare cereal according to package directions using milk; remove from heat. Stir in peaches, almonds, honey, and almond extract. Pour into greased 5 or 6-cup ring mold; cover surface with plastic wrap. Chill until firm, about 2 to 3 hours.

To serve, loosen edges of mold with a knife and invert onto serving platter. Heat raspberry jam until smooth; use to top individual servings.

DESSERT CREPES

Makes 8

Crepes:
- 2 eggs
- 1 cup milk
- 1 cup all-purpose flour
- 2 tablespoons sugar
- 2 tablespoons butter or margarine, melted
- ½ teaspoon salt

Frosting:
- ½ cup sour cream
- 1 teaspoon grated lemon peel
- ½ cup Welch's squeezable strawberry spread
- Sugar or confectioner's sugar

Thoroughly combine eggs, milk, flour, sugar, margarine, and salt. Set aside for 30 minutes.

Place an 8-inch crepe or omelet pan over medium heat (if pan is not seasoned or nonstick coated, add a small amount of butter); when hot, pour in ¼ cup crepe batter. Rotate pan to completely cover the bottom. Cook 1 to 2 minutes or until the one side is golden brown. Turn crepe and allow the opposite side to dry. Remove crepe from pan, reheat pan, and repeat procedure, stacking cooked crepes between sheets of waxed paper.

To serve, mix sour cream with lemon peel. Spread half of the unbrowned side of each crepe with 1 tablespoon sour cream mixture and the other half of each crepe with 1 tablespoon strawberry spread. Fold crepe in half, then in half again creating a triangle. If desired, sprinkle with sugar or confectioner's sugar.

ORANGE CREAMSICAL DESSERT

Makes 12 servings

two 3-ounce packages Royal® orange gelatin

1 cup boiling water

½ cup cold water

two 3⅜-ounce packages Royal® instant vanilla pudding and pie filling

2 cups cold milk

two 11-ounce cans mandarin oranges, drained

2 cups prepared whipped topping

Lime peel, for garnish

In small bowl, dissolve gelatin in boiling water; stir in cold water. Chill until slightly thickened.

Prepare pudding according to package directions using milk. Reserve 5 mandarin oranges for garnish. Fold remaining mandarin oranges, thickened gelatin, and 1 cup whipped topping into prepared pudding. Pour into 6-cup ring mold. Chill 4 hours or until set.

To serve, unmold onto serving plate. Spoon remaining whipped topping in center of ring. Garnish with reserved mandarin oranges and lime peel cut into leaf shapes.

CHOCOLATE-PEANUT PARFAIT

Makes 6 servings

13-ounce package
   Royal® no
   bake chocolate
   peanut butter
   pie
½ cup chopped
   honey roasted
   peanuts

⅓ cup margarine,
   melted
1 tablespoon sugar
1¼ cups plus ⅓ cup
   cold milk
Prepared
   whipped
   topping, for
   garnish

Combine crumb packet, nuts, margarine, and sugar; set aside. Separately prepare peanut butter filling and chocolate topping according to package directions using milk.

Spoon about 2 tablespoons peanut butter filling into each of six 6-ounce parfait glasses. Top each with 2 tablespoons crumb mixture. Divide and layer chocolate topping, remaining crumb mixture, and peanut butter filling among parfaits. Chill at least 2 hours. Garnish with whipped topping if desired.

JELLY SURPRISES

Makes 4 cones

¼ cup peanut
    butter
¼ cup Welch's
    jelly

1 pint vanilla ice
    cream, softened
4 ice cream cones

Swirl peanut butter and jelly into ice cream. Refreeze for at least 4 hours or until ice cream is hard again.

When ready to serve, squeeze 1 teaspoon jelly into tip of cone. Top with peanut butter and jelly ice cream.

YOGURT POPS

Makes 4 pops

8-ounce
    container
    vanilla
    yogurt

4 tablespoons
    Welch's
    strawberry or
    raspberry apple
    spread

Evenly divide yogurt into four 3-ounce paper cups. Swirl in about 1 tablespoon spread into each. Freeze 1 hour.

When partially set, insert wooden stick. Freeze until firm. To eat, peel away paper cup.

Beverages

APPLE-APRICOT PUNCH

Makes six 8-ounce servings

2 cups water
  12-ounce can
    apricot nectar
  6-ounce can
    Seneca frozen
    concentrated
    apple juice, thawed

¼ cup sugar
  Ice cubes
  28-ounce bottle
    ginger ale,
    chilled

In bowl, combine water, nectar, apple juice concentrate, and sugar. Stir until dissolved. Pour over ice in punch bowl. Pour in ginger ale; stir to mix.

CREAMY MOCHA BEVERAGE

Makes 8 servings

⅔ cup instant
   cocoa mix
½ cup instant
   coffee

8 cups boiling water
Cool Whip®
   whipped topping

Combine cocoa and coffee. Place in serving
pitcher. Pour in boiling water and stir well. Serve
hot in mugs; top with whipped topping.

PEACHY-APPLE COOLER

Makes 4 servings

two 8-ounce
   containers
   peach
   yogurt
  6-ounce can
   Seneca
   frozen
   concentrated
   apple juice

½ teaspoon vanilla
   extract
3 ice cubes

Put all ingredients in blender container; cover.
Blend at high speed for 2 minutes or until mixture
is well combined and ice cubes are reduced to small
pieces. Serve in chilled glasses.

ICE TEA DELIGHT

Makes 8 servings

4 cups strong cold
    tea
3 tablespoons
    Grandma's®
    molasses
    (Gold Label)

1 pint vanilla ice
    cream
Carbonated water

Blend tea and molasses. Fill tall glass half full with mixture. Add a scoop of ice cream. Fill with carbonated water.

PINK CLOUD

Makes 1 serving

1 ripe banana or
    pear, peeled
½ cup Welch's
    white grape
    juice

½ cup vanilla yogurt
22-ounce bottle
    Welch's
    squeezable
    strawberry
    spread

In blender, combine fruit, grape juice, and yogurt. Process until smooth. With blender running, squeeze in about 2 tablespoons of spread. Serve immediately.

Purple Cloud:

Substitute purple grape juice for the white grape juice and use Welch's grape jelly instead of strawberry spread.

GOLDEN PUNCH

Makes 20 6-ounce servings

40-ounce bottle
Welch's
white grape
juice, chilled

12-ounce can
frozen
concentrated
orange juice,
thawed

46-ounce can
pineapple juice,
chilled

33.8-ounce bottle
club soda,
chilled

20 strawberries,
washed and
hulled

20 mint sprigs

Mix together in punch bowl. Add ice ring or ice cubes. Place whole strawberry and mint sprig in each glass before chilling.

TROPICAL SUNRISE

Makes 1 serving

½ cup Welch's
    white grape
    juice
1 tablespoon each
    frozen
    pineapple
    and orange
    juice
    concentrates

2 teaspoons grated
    coconut
4–5 ice cubes
    Pineapple wedge
    and orange
    slice

In container of electric blender combine juice, concentrates, coconut, and ice; blend until smooth.

Serve in tall glass garnished with pineapple wedge and orange slice.

BREAKFAST BEVERAGE

Makes 1 serving

3 tablespoons
    Seneca frozen
    concentrated
    raspberry
    cranberry
    juice cocktail

1 cup cold water
1 egg
1 tablespoon milk

Combine concentrate, water, egg, and milk in container of electric blender. Blend until smooth. Chill. Serve in tall glass.

HOT BUTTERED CRANBERRY COCKTAIL

Makes 8 to 10 servings

4½ cups water
¼ cup sugar
3 sticks cinnamon
1 teaspoon whole cloves

12-ounce can Seneca frozen concentrated cranberry juice
Butter or margarine
Ground nutmeg

In saucepan, combine water, sugar, cinnamon sticks, and cloves. Heat to boiling. Reduce heat; simmer 10 minutes. Strain and discard spices. Add concentrate. Heat gently.

Serve hot. Top each serving with about ½ teaspoon butter or margarine. Sprinkle with nutmeg.

GREAT GRAPE ICE TEA

Makes 9 servings

9 cups boiling water
9 lemon flavored herb tea bags

1⅛ cups Welch's purple grape juice
Mint leaves and lemon slices

Steep tea bags in boiling water for 5 minutes. Remove tea bags. Stir in grape juice. Chill.

Fill tall glasses with ice, fill with tea, and garnish with mint and lemon slices.

Juicy Cubes

Pour Welch's grape juice (purple, red, or white) into ice cube trays; freeze. Use to cool beverages without diluting or use in place of ice cubes in frosty blender drinks.

RASPBERRY–CRANBERRY ICE CREAM SHAKE

Makes 2 servings

6 tablespoons
Seneca frozen
concentrated
raspberry
cranberry
juice cocktail

2 cups vanilla ice
cream
1 tablespoon sugar
1 cup cold milk

Combine all ingredients in container of electric blender. Blend at high speed until smooth.

Brand Name Food Shopping List

Brand Name Products Whose Recipes and/or Money-Saving Coupons Appear in This Cookbook

- Adolph's® Marinade in Minutes
- Carnation® evaporated milk
- Carnation® sweetened condensed milk
- Cool Whip® whipped topping
- Grandma's® molasses
- Heinz chili sauce
- Heinz HomeStyle gravy
- Heinz tomato ketchup
- Heinz vinegar
- Kretschmer® wheat germ
- Lea & Perrins Worcestershire sauce
- Nabisco® Cream of Wheat®
- † Nestlé® Toll House® chocolate morsels

---

*Coupon only.
†Recipes only.

* Quaker Oven Stuffs®
* Quaker rice cakes
† Reynolds cooking bags
• Royal® gelatin and pudding and No Bake pie mix
• Seneca frozen cranberry juice
• Shady Brook Farms® turkey
• Welch's grape juice
• Welch's spreads

Something for the Cook's Kitchen

From Farberware, Inc.

Farberware® indoor smokeless grill
Farberware® electric skillet
Farberware® electric wok
*Farberware® convection oven

From Sears "Kenmore Choice" line

"Brew for Two" 12-cup coffeemaker
*Deluxe 14-speed blender
*Toaster oven broiler
*Food processor and others

Money-Saving
Coupons Section

You've got it made with
Marinade in Minutes

MANUFACTURER COUPON
EXPIRES 10/31/1996
30¢
30¢ OFF
HEINZ
KETCHUP
ANY SIZE. ANY VARIETY.
30¢
EASY SQUEEZE
HEINZ
TOMATO
KETCHUP

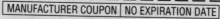

15483

5 41800 10020 5

15713

5 41800 60020 0

35¢ OFF
ANY
Quaker
Rice
Cakes

19202

5 30000 56035 3

SAVE 15¢
ON ANY SIZE TUB OF

CoolWhip
WHIPPED TOPPING

Homemade
Fresh Taste

CoolWhip
NON-DAIRY
WHIPPED TOPPING
ONLY 12 CALORIES

GFH78481TØ

30

5 43000 26115 1

MANUFACTURER'S COUPON / NO EXPIRATION DATE

SAVE 15¢

on any size
GRANDMA'S® MOLASSES

154545

RETAILER: One coupon per purchase of product indicated. Consumer to pay sales tax. Cadbury Beverages Inc. will reimburse you for the face value plus 8¢ handling, if submitted in compliance with Cadbury Beverages Inc. Coupon Redemption Policy incorporated herein by reference. For free copy and/or coupon redemption, send to: Mott's U.S.A., a division of Cadbury Beverages Inc., P.O. Box 880046, El Paso, Texas 88588-0046. Cash value 1/20 of 1¢.

5 14800 30015 9

*Surprise! Grandma's®
Molasses is great for more
than baking. Try it in
barbecue sauces, salads—
wherever you need a little
natural sweetness.*

**THE "SURPRISE"
NATURAL SWEETENER®**

MANUFACTURER COUPON
EXPIRES 10/31/96
30¢
30¢ OFF
ONE JAR
HEINZ
GRAVY
ANY SIZE
ANY FLAVOR
30¢
Brown
HEINZ
HomeStyle
Gravy
Brown

Save 25¢ on any variety
of Seneca Frozen Cranberry Juice

5   37100 15625   7

50192

Seneca - the juice family for your whole family!

SAVE 35¢

On **ONE** 14 oz. can of

Carnation®

SWEETENED CONDENSED MILK

VALUABLE COUPON ON BACK

SAVE 10¢

On **TWO** 12 fl. oz. cans of

Carnation®

EVAPORATED MILK
(Any Variety)

VALUABLE COUPON ON BACK

MANUFACTURER COUPON | **EXPIRES 10/31/96**

30¢

30¢ OFF
HEINZ
VINEGAR
ANY SIZE

HEINZ
DISTILLED
WHITE
VINEGAR
5% Acidity

HEINZ
DISTILLED
WHITE
VINEGAR
5% Acidity

30¢

30¢

43268

5 13000 62130 9

MONEY SAVERS
Mail-In-Coupon
SAVE $5.00

ON

Farberware®
Indoor Smokeless Grill
MODEL #R 4550 or R 4500
(See coupon back for details)

Mail-In-Coupon

THIS COUPON WORTH $5 OFF FARBERWARE® INDOOR SMOKELESS GRILL

MODEL # R 4550 or R 4500

To obtain your $5 rebate, mail this coupon with Proof of Purchase Sales Slip, carton label showing Model # and Bar Code to:

FARBERWARE® INC., c/o C.K. Enterprises P.O. Box 98, Suffern, NY 10901

Name _____

Address: _____

City: _____ State ___ Zip _____

Offer good in U.S.A. and Canada. One coupon per purchase. Void where prohibited. May not be used in conjunction with any other offer or coupon. Allow 6-8 weeks for receipt of rebate.

MONEY SAVERS
Mail-In-Coupon
SAVE $5⁰⁰

ON

Farberware®
Electric Skillet
MODEL #344A or B 3000
(See coupon back for details)

Mail-In-Coupon

THIS COUPON WORTH **$5** OFF FARBERWARE®
ELECTRIC SKILLET

MODEL #344A or B 3000

To obtain your $5 rebate, mail this coupon with Proof of Purchase Sales Slip, carton label showing Model # and Bar Code to:

FARBERWARE® INC., c/o C.K. Enterprises P.O. Box 98, Suffern, NY 10901

Name _____

Address: _____

City: _____ State ____ Zip _____

Offer good in U.S.A. and Canada. One coupon per purchase. Void where prohibited. May not be used in conjunction with any other offer or coupon. Allow 6-8 weeks for receipt of rebate.

MONEY SAVERS
Mail-In-Coupon
SAVE $5⁰⁰

ON

Farberware®
Electric Wok
MODEL #343A or B 2000
(See coupon back for details)

Mail-In-Coupon

THIS COUPON WORTH $5 OFF FARBERWARE® ELECTRIC WOK

MODEL #343 A or B 2000

To obtain your $5 rebate, mail this coupon with Proof of Purchase Sales Slip, carton label showing Model # and Bar Code to:

FARBERWARE® INC., c/o C.K. Enterprises P.O. Box 98, Suffern, NY 10901

Name _____

Address: _____

City: _____ State ____ Zip _____

Offer good in U.S.A. and Canada. One coupon per purchase. Void where prohibited. May not be used in conjunction with any other offer or coupon. Allow 6-8 weeks for receipt of rebate.

MONEY SAVERS
Mail-In-Coupon
SAVE $10⁰⁰

ON

Farberware®
Convection Oven
MODEL # T 4800 or T 4850
(See coupon back for details)

Mail-In-Coupon

THIS COUPON WORTH $10 OFF FARBERWARE® CONVECTION OVEN®

MODEL #T 4800 or T 4850

To obtain your $10 rebate, mail this coupon with Proof of Purchase Sales Slip, carton label showing Model # and Bar Code to:

FARBERWARE® INC., c/o C.K. Enterprises P.O. Box 98, Suffern, NY 10901

Name _____

Address: _____

City: _____ State ___ Zip _____

Offer good in U.S.A. and Canada. One coupon per purchase. Void where prohibited. May not be used in conjunction with any other offer or coupon. Allow 6-8 weeks for receipt of rebate.

Index